EASTER SEASON REFLECTIONS FOR NEW CATHOLICS

Dennis Chriszt, C.PP.S.

*To*_____

*From*_____

_____

EASTER SEASON REFLECTIONS FOR NEW CATHOLICS

Author: Dennis Chriszt, C.PP.S.
Editor: Jerry Galipeau
Copy Editor: Marcia T. Lucey
Cover and Book Design: Chris Broquet
Editorial Director: Mary Beth Kunde-Anderson
Production Manager: Deb Johnston
Art: Michael O'Neill McGrath, OSFS

The Fifty Days of Joy: Easter Season Reflections for New Catholics © 2006, World Library Publications, the music and liturgy division of J. S. Paluch Company, Inc., 3708 River Road, Suite 400, Franklin Park, Illinois 60131-2158.

Excerpts from the Lectionary for Mass for use in the Dioceses of the United States of America, second typical edition Copyright © 2001, 1997, 1986, 1970 by the Confraternity of Christian Doctrine, Inc., Washington DC. Used with permission. All rights reserved. No portion of this text may be reproduced by any means without permission in writing from the copyright owner.

Excerpts from the The New American Bible with Revised New Testament and Psalms Copyright © 1991, 1986, 1970 by the Confraternity of Christian Doctrine, Inc., Washington DC. Used with permission. All rights reserved. No portion of the New American Bible may be reproduced by any means without permission in writing from the copyright owner.

Excerpts from the English translation of The Roman Missal Copyright © 1973, International Committee on English in the Liturgy, Inc. (ICEL); excerpts from the English translation of Rite of Christian Initiation of Adults © 1985, (ICEL). All rights reserved.

Copyright © 2006, World Library Publications, the music and liturgy division of J.S. Paluch Company, Inc. 3708 River Road, Suite 400, Franklin Park, IL 60131-2158. All rights reserved.

Artwork by Michael O'Neill McGrath, OSFS. Copyright © 2001, 2002, 2006, World Library Publications.

World Library Publications
the music and liturgy division of J.S. Paluch Company, Inc.
3708 River Road, Suite 400
Franklin Park, Illinois 60131-2158
800 566-6150
wlpcs@jspaluch.com • www.wlpmusic.com

TABLE OF CONTENTS

Introduction 4
How to Use this Book 5
Easter Week
    Easter Sunday 7
    Easter Monday 10
    Easter Tuesday 18
    Easter Wednesday 26
    Easter Thursday 30
    Easter Friday 35
    Easter Saturday 42

Sundays of the Easter Season
    Second Sunday of Easter *(Years A, B, & C)* 48
    Third Sunday of Easter *(Years A, B, & C)* 53
    Fourth Sunday of Easter *(Years A, B, & C)* 61
    Fifth Sunday of Easter *(Year A)* 67
    Fifth Sunday of Easter *(Year B)* 70
    Fifth Sunday of Easter *(Year C)* 73
    Sixth Sunday of Easter *(Years A & C)* 77
    Sixth Sunday of Easter *(Year B)* 81
    Ascension of the Lord *(Years A, B, & C)* 85
    Seventh Sunday of Easter *(Years A, B, & C)* 90
    Pentecost *(Years A, B, & C)* 93

INTRODUCTION

Once upon a time, long, long ago (way back in the late fourth century) and far, far away (in places like Milan, Jerusalem, Antioch, and Mopsuestia) there was mystagogy. It primarily consisted of sermons or homilies preached by men like Ambrose, Cyril, John Chrysostom, and Theodore. Then and there, these great preachers met with the newly baptized and shared their reflections on what it meant to be a Christian. These reflections always began with their experiences, especially the experiences of the sacraments of initiation—what they called the mysteries. They included references to the scriptures and to other common experiences that might help shed light on the meaning of the mysteries they had recently experienced.

This book grows out of the experience of those fourth-century mystagogues, as well as the experience of twenty-five neophytes I interviewed as part of the research I did for my doctoral thesis project. It grows out of over twenty years of preaching, presiding at liturgy, and training others for ministry with the Rite of Christian Initiation of Adults, as well as my own experience of life and of the sacraments.

The reflections in this book are first and foremost meant to be used by neophytes, those who have just been baptized. Those who have recently been received into the Church or who have completed their Christian initiation will also find this book helpful. It can also be useful for any baptized Christian who seeks to grow in his or her own faith throughout the Easter season.

You may wish to use this book in your own personal reflections. You might also want to use this book in conversation with your godparent or sponsor as you meet together throughout the Easter season. You might find the book helpful in a group setting when other neophytes, godparents, sponsors, and mystagogues (catechists for post-baptismal catechesis) gather together.

This book is meant to help you develop a pattern of reflection, beginning with your own experience both in the normal events of life and in the mysteries we call the sacraments. It begins with reflections for each day of Easter week, reflections based on the experience of the Easter Vigil. It continues with reflections that find their focus in the Sunday celebrations of the Eucharist during the Easter season—the place where, the Church tells us, mystagogy takes place.

Each reflection is meant to bring your experience, the word of God, and the Church's tradition into conversation with one another in order to deepen your faith, your understanding of that faith, and your response to the gift of faith that you have received. For each reader, that response will be different, because the experiences of life will have been different. The questions that are part of each reflection have no single answers. Your own answers will grow out of an open interchange between your experience, the Church's tradition, and the God who has been part of both.

It is my hope that these reflections will help you discover that unique way in which you have been called by God to respond to the gift of faith received.

May God continue to bless you and walk with you as you seek to make the most of mystagogy during the Fifty Days of joy.

Dennis Chriszt, C.PP.S.

HOW TO USE THIS BOOK

This book is meant to help you develop a pattern of reflection, beginning with your own experience both in the normal events of life and in the mysteries we call the sacraments. It begins with entries for each day of Easter week, based on the experience of the Easter Vigil. It continues with entries that find their focus in the Sunday celebrations of the Eucharist during the Easter season—the place where, the Church tells us, mystagogy takes place.

The Church gives us a three-year cycle of readings in order to open up the riches of the bible. You will notice that in this book some Sundays of the Easter Season are designated by liturgical year, using the letters 'A,' 'B,' and 'C.' For some Sundays, there is one entry for all three years. Others are designated according to year. The following chart lists the liturgical year (A, B, or C) that corresponds to the calendar year.

    2007 – Year C
    2008 – Year A
    2009 – Year B
    2010 – Year C
    2011 – Year A
    2012 – Year B
    2013 – Year C
    2014 – Year A
    2015 – Year B
    2016 – Year C

Easter Sunday

REMEMBERING

We begin by remembering. We remember events long ago and not so long ago. We remember that first Easter morning. We remember our first Easter morning as fully initiated Catholic Christians.

READING

John 20:1–9

On the first day of the week, Mary of Magdala came to the tomb early in the morning, while it was still dark, and saw the stone removed from the tomb. So she ran and went to Simon Peter and to the other disciple whom Jesus loved, and told them, "They have taken the Lord from the tomb, and we don't know where they put him." So Peter and the other disciple went out and came to the tomb. They both ran, but the other disciple ran faster than Peter and arrived at the tomb first; he bent down and saw the burial cloths there, but did not go in. When Simon Peter arrived after him, he went into the tomb and saw the burial cloths there, and the cloth that had covered his head, not with the burial cloths but rolled up in a separate place. Then the other disciple also went in, the one who had arrived at the tomb first, and he saw and believed. For they did not yet understand the Scripture that he had to rise from the dead.

REMEMBERING

We remember that the disciples hadn't understood what Jesus was saying when he told them that the Son of Man would have to suffer, die, and rise again on the third day. We remember how puzzled they were whenever he spoke of death and resurrection. They remembered what had just happened—how they had only recently entered Jerusalem victoriously, had gathered to celebrate the Passover with the Lord a few days later, and had witnessed his arrest, trial, and execution. They remembered the fear and the sense of failure as they saw their hopes and dreams dashed by the Master's death. And as they stood at the tomb, they remembered all of that, and seeing it empty, they somehow believed.

REFLECTING

What must they have been thinking when Mary of Magdala first approached them with the news that the tomb was empty? What would you have felt at such news? What would you have thought as you ran there? What would you have thought or felt as you saw that it was true? What would you have said to the others as you returned to the upper room?

REMEMBERING

We remember what happened last night. We remember gathering in darkness. We remember the fire and light, the stories, the water, the white garments, the oil, the bread and wine. We remember the people—all who had major roles to play in the celebration, as well as those who participated in it with us. We remember sponsors and godparents, family and friends who gathered with us. We remember strangers who gathered and prayed with us, too. We remember the stories, the songs, the music, and the aromas of incense and sacred chrism. We remember all the feelings associated with what had happened.

REFLECTING

What were the highlights of last evening? What words stand out? What actions? What ritual elements? What feelings? If you had to describe the event in one or two sentences, what would you say? How would you describe it to another member of the Church? How would you describe it to a stranger to the faith?

READING

John 20:11–18

Mary Magdalen stayed outside the tomb weeping. And as she wept, she bent over into the tomb and saw two angels in white sitting there, one at the head and one at the feet where the Body of Jesus had been. And they said to her, "Woman, why are you weeping?" She said to them, "They have taken my Lord, and I don't know where they laid him." When she had said this, she turned around and saw Jesus there, but did not know it was Jesus. Jesus said to her, "Woman, why are you weeping? Whom are you looking for?" She thought it was the gardener and said to him, "Sir, if you carried him away, tell me where you laid him, and I will take him." Jesus said to her, "Mary!" She turned and said to him in Hebrew, "Rabbouni," which means Teacher. Jesus said to her, "Stop holding on to me, for I have not yet ascended to the Father. But go to my brothers and tell them, 'I am going to my Father and your Father, to my God and your God.'" Mary of Magdala went and announced to the disciples, "I have seen the Lord," and then reported what he had told her.

REMEMBERING

We remember what it must have been like for Mary. She had seen the Lord. She must have wondered, "Did it really happen the way I remember it?" She must have looked back with an overwhelming sense of joy. She didn't recognize him at first. But when she heard him call her by name, she knew.

REFLECTING

How was she to describe her experience to others? How would you describe such an experience? What would you do next? Where would you go? What would you say?

PRAYING

Offer a prayer of thanks to God for what you have experienced.

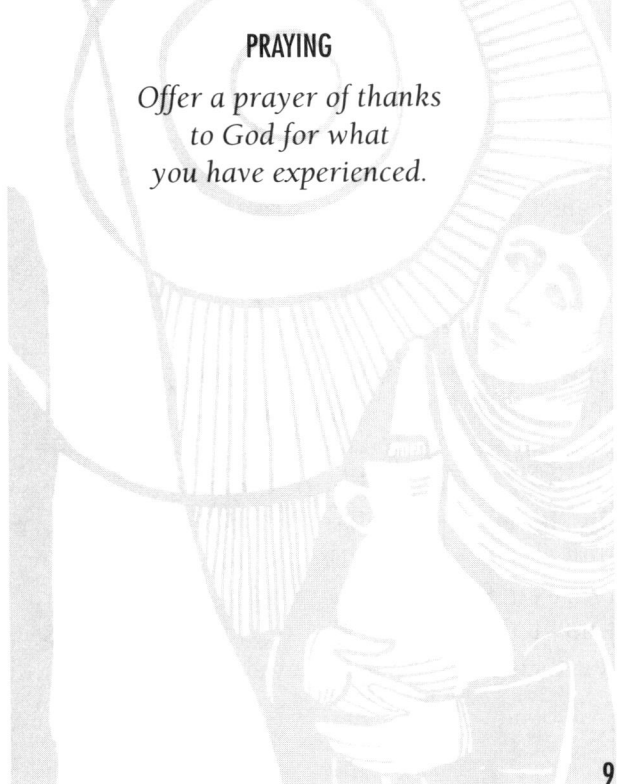

Easter Monday

Place a single candle as a focal point for your reflection. When gathering in a large group, gather around the Easter Candle. In a smaller group or by yourself, use the candle you received at your baptism at the Easter Vigil.

REMEMBERING

We begin by remembering. We remember events long ago and not so long ago. We remember being scared of the dark. We remember staring at the sky on a particularly clear night when stars were in abundance. We remember a single candle burning in a dark room. We remember the comfort brought by that light.

We remember the flames of the Easter fire. We remember the Easter candle being blessed and lit. We remember the spreading of the light as candle after candle was lit from that single flame. We remember the words sung by the light of those candles: "Rejoice, heavenly powers! Sing, choirs of angels! Exult, all creation around God's throne! Jesus Christ, our King, is risen!"

We remember that night long, long ago, when God's word was first spoken: "Let there be light." And there was light!

The author of the first creation story (Genesis 1:1 — 2:4) tells us that light was created first. Nuclear physicists tell us it all began with a brilliant light as the Big Bang exploded on the scene and the universe was born. Light—the first energy released in creation—is still, with all our knowledge, a bit of a mystery. Scientists tell us it behaves as both particle and wave.

REFLECTING

What memories of light and darkness do you bring with you today? What are your memories of darkness? What are your memories of candles burning in the night? What feelings do these memories evoke?

Reflect on your experience of the Easter Vigil. What was your experience as the light from the Easter candle was brought into the church? What was your experience as the light spread throughout the assembly? What was it like to be one of the few who did not hold such a candle at that moment? What was it like when you were given a candle later in the liturgy?

Its energy is transformed by plants into food and nourishment for other forms of life. It warms and transforms. Some anthropologists would say that when humanity learned to control light (fire), we achieved something astonishing, something that sets us apart from every other creature.

On Saturday night, as we gathered for the Easter Vigil, we gathered in darkness. A fire was lit and blessed. A huge candle was blessed and lit. And from the single flame of that one candle others were lit until the whole church was ablaze with the light that overcame the darkness.

It is no accident that both the Incarnation and the Resurrection occur at night. Christmas and Easter begin in darkness, and suddenly there is light. There is the light of the stars that first Christmas night, stars that led others to discover that the Light of the World had been born among us. There is the light of a new dawn, as the tomb bursts open and Christ's light shines for all to see.

All these memories of light and darkness, of the light overcoming the darkness, are the foundation for this reflection.

READING

Genesis 1:1 — 2:4

In the beginning, when God created the heavens and the earth, the earth was a formless wasteland, and darkness covered the abyss, while a mighty wind swept over the waters.

Then God said, "Let there be light," and there was light. God saw how good the light was. God then separated the light from the darkness. God called the light "day," and the darkness he called "night." Thus evening came, and morning followed—the first day.

Then God said, "Let there be a dome in the middle of the waters, to separate one body of water from the other." And so it happened: God made the dome, and it separated the water above the dome from the water below it. God called the dome "the sky." Evening came, and morning followed—the second day.

Then God said, "Let the water under the sky be gathered into a single basin, so that the dry land may appear." And so it happened: the water under the sky was gathered into its basin, and the dry land appeared. God called the dry land "the earth," and the basin of the water he called "the sea." God saw how good it was. Then God said, "Let the earth bring forth vegetation: every kind of plant that bears seed and every kind of fruit tree on earth that bears fruit with its seed in it." And so it happened: the earth brought forth every kind of plant that bears seed and every kind of fruit tree on earth that bears fruit with its seed in it. God saw how good it was. Evening came, and morning followed—the third day.

Then God said: "Let there be lights in the dome of the sky, to separate day from night. Let them mark the fixed times, the days and the years, and serve as luminaries in the dome of the sky, to shed light upon the earth." And so it happened: God made the two great lights, the greater one to govern the day, and the lesser one to govern the night; and he made the stars. God set them in the dome of the sky, to shed light upon the earth, to govern the day and the night, and to separate the light from the darkness. God saw how good it was. Evening came, and morning followed—the fourth day.

Then God said, "Let the water teem with an abundance of living creatures, and on the earth let birds fly beneath the dome of the sky." And so it happened: God created the great sea monsters and all kinds of swimming creatures with which the water teems, and all kinds of winged birds. God saw how good it was, and God blessed them, saying, "Be fertile, multiply, and fill the water of the seas; and let the birds multiply on the earth." Evening came, and morning followed—the fifth day.

Then God said, "Let the earth bring forth all kinds of living creatures: cattle, creeping things, and wild animals of all kinds." And so it happened: God made all kinds of wild animals, all kinds of cattle, and all kinds of creeping things of the earth. God saw how good it was. Then God said: "Let us make man in our image, after our likeness. Let them have dominion over the fish of the sea, the birds of the air, and the cattle, and over all the wild animals and all the creatures that crawl on the ground."

PRAYING
Psalm 27:1–2, 4, 13–14

*The LORD is my light and
my salvation;
whom do I fear?
The LORD is my life's refuge;
of whom am I afraid?
When evildoers come at me
to devour my flesh,
These my enemies and foes
themselves stumble
and fall.*

*One thing I ask of the LORD;
this I seek:
To dwell in the LORD's house
all the days of my life,
To gaze on the LORD's
beauty,
to visit his temple.*

*But I believe I shall enjoy
the LORD's goodness
in the land of the
living.
Wait for the LORD,
take courage;
be stouthearted,
wait for the LORD!*

God created man in his image;
in the image of God he created him;
male and female he created them.

God blessed them, saying: "Be fertile and multiply; fill the earth and subdue it. Have dominion over the fish of the sea, the birds of the air, and all the living things that move on the earth." God also said: "See, I give you every seed-bearing plant all over the earth and every tree that has seed-bearing fruit on it to be your food; and to all the animals of the land, all the birds of the air, and all the living creatures that crawl on the ground, I give all the green plants for food." And so it happened. God looked at everything he had made, and he found it very good. Evening came, and morning followed—the sixth day.

Thus the heavens and the earth and all their array were completed. Since on the seventh day God was finished with the work he had been doing, he rested on the seventh day from all the work he had undertaken.

READING

Read about the Light. Choose any of the following readings:

John 1:1–18

>In the beginning was the Word,
>>and the Word was with God,
>>and the Word was God.
>
>He was in the beginning with God.
>All things came to be through him,
>>and without him nothing came to be.
>
>What came to be through him was life,
>>and this life was the light of the human race;
>
>the light shines in the darkness,
>>and the darkness has not overcome it.

A man named John was sent from God. He came for testimony, to testify to the light, so that all might believe through him. He was not the light, but came to testify to the light. The true light, which enlightens everyone, was coming into the world.

>He was in the world,
>>and the world came to be through him,
>>but the world did not know him.
>
>He came to what was his own,
>>but his own people did not accept him.

But to those who did accept him he gave power to become children of God, to those who believe in his name, who were born not by natural generation nor by human choice nor by a man's decision but of God.

>And the Word became flesh
>>and made his dwelling among us,
>>and we saw his glory,
>>the glory as of the Father's only Son,
>>full of grace and truth.

John testified to him and cried out, saying, "This was he of whom I said, 'The one who is coming after me ranks ahead of me because he existed before me.'" From his fullness we have all received, grace in place of grace, because while the law was given through Moses, grace and truth came through Jesus Christ. No one has ever seen God. The only Son, God, who is at the Father's side, has revealed him.

John 3:16–21
God so loved the world that he gave his only-begotten Son, so that everyone who believes in him might not perish but might have eternal life. For God did not send his Son into the world to condemn the world, but that the world might be saved through him. Whoever believes in him will not be condemned, but whoever does not believe has already been condemned, because he has not believed in the name of the only-begotten Son of God. And this is the verdict, that the light came into the world, but people preferred darkness to light, because their works were evil. For everyone who does wicked things hates the light and does not come toward the light, so that his works might not be exposed. But whoever lives the truth comes to the light, so that his works may be clearly seen as done in God.

John 8:12
Jesus spoke to them again, saying, "I am the light of the world. Whoever follows me will not walk in darkness, but will have the light of life."

John 9:1–7
As Jesus passed by he saw a man blind from birth. His disciples asked him, "Rabbi, who sinned, this man or his parents, that he was born blind?" Jesus answered, "Neither he nor his parents sinned; it is so that the works of God might be made visible through him. We have to do the works of the one who sent me while it is day. Night is coming when no one can work. While I am in the world, I am the light of the world." When he had said this, he spat on the ground and made clay with the saliva, and smeared the clay on his eyes, and said to him, "Go wash in the Pool of Siloam" —which means Sent—. So he went and washed, and came back able to see.

John 12:35–36, 46
Jesus said to them, "The light will be among you only a little while. Walk while you have the light, so that darkness may not overcome you. Whoever walks in the dark does not know where he is going. While you have the light, believe in the light, so that you may become children of the light."

"I came into the world as light, so that everyone who believes in me might not remain in darkness."

REFLECTING

How has Jesus been a light for you? What darkness has he overcome?

READING

Read about living in the light. Choose any of the following readings:

Matthew 5:14–16

You are the light of the world. A city set on a mountain cannot be hidden. Nor do they light a lamp and then put it under a bushel basket; it is set on a lampstand, where it gives light to all in the house. Just so, your light must shine before others, that they may see your good deeds and glorify your heavenly Father.

Ephesians 5:8–9

You were once darkness, but now you are light in the Lord. Live as children of light, for light produces every kind of goodness and righteousness and truth.

1 Peter 2:9

You are "a chosen race, a royal priesthood,
   a holy nation, a people of his own,
   so that you may announce the praises" of him
   who called you out of darkness into his wonderful light.

1 John 1:5–7

Beloved: This is the message that we have heard from Jesus Christ and proclaim to you: God is light, and in him there is no darkness at all. If we say, "We have fellowship with God," while we continue to walk in darkness, we lie and do not act in truth. But if we walk in the light as he is in the light, then we have fellowship with one another, and the Blood of his Son Jesus cleanses us from all sin.

1 John 2:7–11

Beloved, I am writing no new commandment to you but an old commandment that you had from the beginning. The old commandment is the word that you have heard. And yet I do write a new commandment to you, which holds true in him and among you, for the darkness is passing away, and the true light is already shining. Whoever says he is in the light, yet hates his brother, is still in the darkness. Whoever loves his brother remains in the light, and there is nothing in him to cause a fall. Whoever hates his brother is in darkness; he walks in darkness and does not know where he is going because the darkness has blinded his eyes.

REFLECTING

What challenges do you face as you try to be light to the world or to live as a child of the light?

REMEMBERING

After you were baptized, you were presented with a candle of your own, and you heard these words:

> You have been enlightened by Christ.
> Walk always as children of the light
> and keep the flame of faith alive
>   in your hearts.
> When the Lord comes, may you go out
>   to meet him
> with all the saints in the heavenly kingdom.

And you responded:

> Amen.

PRAYING

Pray for the grace you need to live as a child of the light.

Easter Tuesday

When meeting at the church, gather around the baptismal font. When reflecting with a smaller group or by yourself, use a small bowl of water as your focal point. If possible, use water taken from the font where you were baptized. Also include the candle used for yesterday's reflection.

REMEMBERING

We begin by remembering. We remember events long ago and not so long ago. We remember how the creation story began:

> In the beginning, when God created the heavens and the earth, the earth was a formless wasteland, and darkness covered the abyss, while a mighty wind swept over the waters. *(Genesis 1:1–2)*

The water was already there. Water is somehow intimately connected with God and with God's creation. On the second day, God separates the waters above from the waters below, and on the third day, God separates the waters below so that dry land might appear. Scientists tell us that all life on this planet originated in water—in the primeval seas.

We also remember the waters of the great flood—waters that destroy, and at the same time, waters that save those who have been chosen to enter the ark.

We remember the waters of the Sea of Reeds, where the Israelite slaves fleeing their former masters stood in fear, afraid that they might be taken back into slavery, afraid that they might be killed on the spot, afraid that they might drown in the waters in front of them. But we also remember how these waters became a place of salvation, where the Israelites were set free from slavery forever.

We might also remember our first encounter with waters deep enough to drown us. We may have jumped into that deep water without fear or stood at the water's edge, wondering and afraid. We may have been taught to swim by someone who cared enough to teach us how to make water our friend. Perhaps fear may have kept us out of the pool, lake, river, or sea.

We have so many different experiences of water: water for drinking and cooking, for washing and cleaning, for swimming, boating, sailing and skiing—waters flowing, moving in waves, showering down from the heavens. We may have experiences of too much water or not enough. We may have had wonderful or terrifying experiences of water. We may have seen water at one time or another as a thing of great beauty or as something to fear.

REFLECTING

What memories of water do you bring with you today? What feelings do these memories evoke?

Reflecting on your experience of the Easter Vigil: what was your experience as the water was blessed? As you entered the water? As you saw others enter the water? As the water was poured on others or on you? As you dried yourself with a towel?

READING

Read one of more of the following scripture stories:

The first creation story—*Genesis 1:1–2; 6–10*

In the beginning, when God created the heavens and the earth, the earth was a formless wasteland, and darkness covered the abyss, while a mighty wind swept over the waters.

Then God said, "Let there be a dome in the middle of the waters, to separate one body of water from the other." And so it happened: God made the dome, and it separated the water above the dome from the water below it. God called the dome "the sky." Evening came, and morning followed—the second day.

Then God said, "Let the water under the sky be gathered into a single basin, so that the dry land may appear." And so it happened: the water under the sky was gathered into its basin, and the dry land appeared. God called the dry land "the earth," and the basin of the water he called "the sea." God saw how good it was.

The great flood—*Genesis 6:5–9;17*

When the LORD saw how great was man's wickedness on earth, and how no desire that his heart conceived was ever anything but evil, he regretted that he had made man on the earth, and his heart was grieved.

So the LORD said: "I will wipe out from the earth the men whom I have created, and not only the men, but also the beasts and the creeping things and the birds of the air, for I am sorry that I made them." But Noah found favor with the LORD. "I, on my part, am about to bring the flood [waters] on the earth, to destroy everywhere all creatures in which there is the breath of life; everything on earth shall perish."

Crossing the Red Sea—*Exodus 14:10–30a*

Pharaoh was already near when the children of Israel looked up and saw that the Egyptians were on the march in pursuit of them. In great fright they cried out to the LORD. And they complained to Moses, "Were there no burial places in Egypt that you had to bring us out here to die in the desert? Why did you do this to us? Why did you bring us out of Egypt? Did we not tell you this in Egypt, when we said, 'Leave us alone. Let us serve the Egyptians'? Far better for us to be the slaves of the Egyptians than to die in the desert." But Moses answered the people, "Fear not! Stand your ground, and you will see the victory the LORD will win for you today. These Egyptians whom you see today you will never see again. The LORD himself will fight for you; you have only to keep still."

Then the Lord said to Moses, "Why are you crying out to me? Tell the children of Israel to go forward. And you, lift up your staff and, with hand outstretched over the sea, split the sea in two, that the children of Israel may pass through it on dry land. But I will make the Egyptians so obstinate that they will go in after them. Then I will receive glory through Pharaoh and all his army, his chariots and charioteers. The Egyptians shall know that I am the Lord, when I receive glory through Pharaoh and his chariots and charioteers."

The angel of God, who had been leading Israel's camp, now moved and went around behind them. The column of cloud also, leaving the front, took up its place behind them, so that it came between the camp of the Egyptians and that of Israel. But the cloud now became dark, and thus the night passed without the rival camps coming any closer together all night long. Then Moses stretched out his hand over the sea, and the Lord swept the sea with a strong east wind throughout the night and so turned it into dry land. When the water was thus divided, the Israelites marched into the midst of the sea on dry land, with the water like a wall to their right and to their left.

The Egyptians followed in pursuit; all Pharaoh's horses and chariots and charioteers went after them right into the midst of the sea. In the night watch just before dawn the Lord cast through the column of the fiery cloud upon the Egyptian force a glance that threw it into a panic; and he so clogged their chariot wheels that they could hardly drive. With that the Egyptians sounded the retreat before Israel, because the Lord was fighting for them against the Egyptians.

Then the Lord told Moses, "Stretch out your hand over the sea, that the water may flow back upon the Egyptians, upon their chariots and their charioteers." So Moses stretched out his hand over the sea, and at dawn the sea flowed back to its normal depth. The Egyptians were fleeing head on toward the sea, when the Lord hurled them into its midst. As the water flowed back, it covered the chariots and the charioteers of Pharaoh's whole army which had followed the Israelites into the sea. Not a single one of them escaped. But the Israelites had marched on dry land through the midst of the sea, with the water like a wall to their right and to their left. Thus the Lord saved Israel on that day from the power of the Egyptians.

PRAYING

Exodus 15:1b–18
I will sing to the Lord, for he is gloriously triumphant;
    horse and chariot he has cast into the sea.
My strength and my courage is the Lord,
    and he has been my savior.
He is my God, I praise him;
    the God of my father, I extol him.

The Lord is a warrior,
    Lord is his name!
Pharaoh's chariots and army he hurled into the sea;
    the elite of his officers were submerged in the Red Sea.
The flood waters covered them,
    they sank into the depths like a stone.

Your right hand, O Lord, magnificent in power,
    your right hand, O Lord, has shattered the enemy.
In your great majesty you overthrew your adversaries;
    you loosed your wrath to consume them like stubble.
At a breath of your anger the waters piled up,
    the flowing waters stood like a mound,
    the flood waters congealed in the midst of the sea.

The enemy boasted, "I will pursue and overtake them;
    I will divide the spoils and have my fill of them;
    I will draw my sword; my hand shall despoil them!"
When your wind blew, the sea covered them;
    like lead they sank in the mighty waters.

Who is like to you among the gods, O Lord?
    Who is like to you, magnificent in holiness?
O terrible in renown, worker of wonders,
    when you stretched out your right hand,
        the earth swallowed them!
In your mercy you led the people you redeemed;
    in your strength you guided them to your holy dwelling.
The nations heard and quaked;
    anguish gripped the dwellers in Philistia.

Then were the princes of Edom dismayed;
> *trembling seized the chieftains of Moab;*
All the dwellers in Canaan melted away;
> *terror and dread fell upon them.*
By the might of your arm they were frozen like stone,
> *while your people, O Lord, passed over,*
> *while the people you had made your own passed over.*

You brought in the people you redeemed
> *and planted them on the mountain of your inheritance—*
> *the place where you made your seat, O Lord,*
> *the sanctuary, Lord, which your hands established.*
The Lord shall reign forever and ever.

READING

Read about the Baptism of Jesus. Choose any of the following readings:

Matthew 3:13–17

Jesus came from Galilee to John at the Jordan to be baptized by him. John tried to prevent him, saying, "I need to be baptized by you, and yet you are coming to me?" Jesus said to him in reply, "Allow it now, for thus it is fitting for us to fulfill all righteousness." Then he allowed him. After Jesus was baptized, he came up from the water and behold, the heavens were opened for him, and he saw the Spirit of God descending like a dove and coming upon him. And a voice came from the heavens, saying, "This is my beloved Son, with whom I am well pleased."

Mark 1:9–11

It happened in those days that Jesus came from Nazareth of Galilee and was baptized in the Jordan by John. On coming up out of the water he saw the heavens being torn open and the Spirit, like a dove, descending upon him. And a voice came from the heavens, "You are my beloved Son; with you I am well pleased."

Luke 3:21–22

After all the people had been baptized and Jesus also had been baptized and was praying, heaven was opened and the holy Spirit descended upon him in bodily form like a dove. And a voice came from heaven, "You are my beloved Son; with you I am well pleased."

John 1:29–34

John the Baptist saw Jesus coming toward him and said, "Behold, the Lamb of God, who takes away the sin of the world. He is the one of whom I said, 'A man is coming after me who ranks ahead of me because he existed before me.' I did not know him, but the reason why I came baptizing with water was that he might be made known to Israel." John testified further, saying, "I saw the Spirit come down like a dove from heaven and remain upon him. I did not know him, but the one who sent me to baptize with water told me, 'On whomever you see the Spirit come down and remain, he is the one who will baptize with the holy Spirit.' Now I have seen and testified that he is the Son of God."

REMEMBERING

As you were baptized, the minister of baptism said: "I baptize you in the name of the Father, and of the Son, and of the Holy Spirit." What did you experience as that happened? What did it feel like physically, psychologically, spiritually? What memories did it evoke? What feelings are you experiencing now, as you remember that moment?

Whether you heard it or not, as you were baptized, the Father in heaven said, "You are my beloved, with whom I am well pleased" (see *Matthew 28:18–20, Mark 16:15–16*).

How would you respond if you had heard the voice as clearly as Jesus did? What difference does it make that you are one of God's beloved children, one of those with whom God is well pleased?

PRAYING

Pray for the grace you need to live as one of God's beloved children.

Easter Wednesday

Wear the white garment that was given to you at your baptism or place a white cloth on a table with the candle and bowl of water used earlier in the week.

REMEMBERING

We begin by remembering. We remember events long ago and not so long ago. We remember how Jesus' body was taken down from the cross and wrapped in a white cloth. We remember that the disciples went to the tomb and discovered the cloth neatly folded and lying there.

We may remember the white baptismal garment worn by an infant who was being baptized, or the white dress worn by a young girl on her First Communion day, or the white gown worn by the bride at a wedding. We might remember new clothes bought for us for a special occasion—for Christmas or Easter, for a wedding or a funeral. We may recall the first time we wore a formal dress or tuxedo—clothing we would wear only once for a special occasion like a prom or a wedding or for some other formal event. We may recall shopping or being measured for those special clothes. We might remember helping a friend or a child of our own as they purchased or rented such clothes for the first time. We might remember having to wear a uniform

REFLECTING

What memories of new clothing do you bring with you today? What feelings do these memories evoke?

Reflect on your experience of the Easter Vigil. What was your experience as you were robed in a white garment? Did someone help you don the robe or did you do it yourself? What was it like to be dressed differently from the way you were dressed when you arrived at church that night? What was it like being dressed differently from the way everyone else in church was dressed? How did you feel at that moment? Looking back at that moment, how do you feel now?

to school, to work, or in the military. We might remember how that uniform made us feel. We might remember the feeling we had when we saw someone we cared about all dressed up in formal attire for the first time. We may recall the first time we saw a minister in liturgical vesture or a person in some kind of uniform. We might remember seeing someone dressed in a particular way that evoked feelings of wonder, awe, or even fear.

We remember the old saying, "The clothes make the man (or woman)." Remember a time when a change in the way someone dressed changed your impression of that person—or how by changing the way you dressed you experienced the fact that people treated you differently.

READING

Read about clothing. Choose any of the following readings.

John 20:1–9

On the first day of the week, Mary of Magdala came to the tomb early in the morning, while it was still dark, and saw the stone removed from the tomb. So she ran and went to Simon Peter and to the other disciple whom Jesus loved, and told them, "They have taken the Lord from the tomb, and we don't know where they put him." So Peter and the other disciple went out and came to the tomb. They both ran, but the other disciple ran faster than Peter and arrived at the tomb first; he bent down and saw the burial cloths there, but did not go in. When Simon Peter arrived after him, he went into the tomb and saw the burial cloths there, and the cloth that had covered his head, not with the burial cloths but rolled up in a separate place. Then the other disciple also went in, the one who had arrived at the tomb first, and he saw and believed. For they did not yet understand the Scripture that he had to rise from the dead.

Romans 13:11–14
    Brothers and sisters: You know the time; it is the hour now for you to awake from sleep. For our salvation is nearer now than when we first believed; the night is advanced, the day is at hand. Let us then throw off the works of darkness and put on the armor of light; let us conduct ourselves properly as in the day, not in orgies and drunkenness, not in promiscuity and lust, not in rivalry and jealousy. But put on the Lord Jesus Christ, and make no provision for the desires of the flesh.

Ephesians 6:10–20
    Brothers and sisters: Draw your strength from the Lord and from his mighty power. Put on the armor of God so that you may be able to stand firm against the tactics of the Devil. For our struggle is not with flesh and blood but with the principalities, with the powers, with the world rulers of this present darkness, with the evil spirits in the heavens. Therefore, put on the armor of God, that you may be able to resist on the evil day and, having done everything, to hold your ground. So stand fast with your loins girded in truth, clothed with righteousness as a breastplate, and your feet shod in readiness for the Gospel of peace. In all circumstances, hold faith as a shield, to quench all [the] flaming arrows of the Evil One. And take the helmet of salvation and the sword of the Spirit, which is the word of God.
    With all prayer and supplication, pray at every opportunity in the Spirit. To that end, be watchful with all perseverance and supplication for all the holy ones and also for me, that speech may be given me to open my mouth, to make known with boldness the mystery of the Gospel for which I am an ambassador in chains, so that I may have the courage to speak as I must.

Colossians 3:12–17
    Brothers and sisters: Put on, as God's chosen ones, holy and beloved, heartfelt compassion, kindness, humility, gentleness, and patience, bearing with one another and forgiving one another, if one has a grievance against another; as the Lord has forgiven you, so must you also do. And over all these put on love, that is, the bond of perfection. And let the peace of Christ control your hearts, the peace into which you were also called in one Body. And be thankful. Let the word of Christ dwell in you richly, as in all wisdom you teach and admonish one another, singing psalms, hymns, and spiritual songs with gratitude in your hearts to God. And whatever you do, in word or in deed, do everything in the name of the Lord Jesus, giving thanks to God the Father through him.

PRAYING

Pray for the grace you need so that others might recognize you as one who is clothed in Christ.

REMEMBERING

As you were being vested or returning to the church in new clothing, the priest may have said this or something like this:

> You have become a new creation
> and have clothed yourself in Christ.
> Receive this baptismal garment
> and bring it unstained to the
>   judgment seat of
>   our Lord Jesus Christ,
> so that you may have everlasting life.

What did you experience as that happened?

REFLECTING

How do you "wear" Christ? What can you do so that others might recognize the Christ you wear?
How do you see others wearing Christ?

Easter Thursday

Use a small vessel of olive oil as a focal point for your reflection. The other items from earlier in the week might also be present.

REMEMBERING

We begin by remembering. We remember events long ago and not so long ago. We remember the oil or ointments that we have used throughout our lives. We may remember the baby oil or Vaseline™ rubbed on a baby's bottom to protect the child from rashes. We may recall using Vicks VapoRub™ to help clear our breathing passages. We might have used hand lotions on dry skin or medicinal ointments on rashes or infections. We may have been massaged with oil that relaxed our muscles and quieted our spirits.

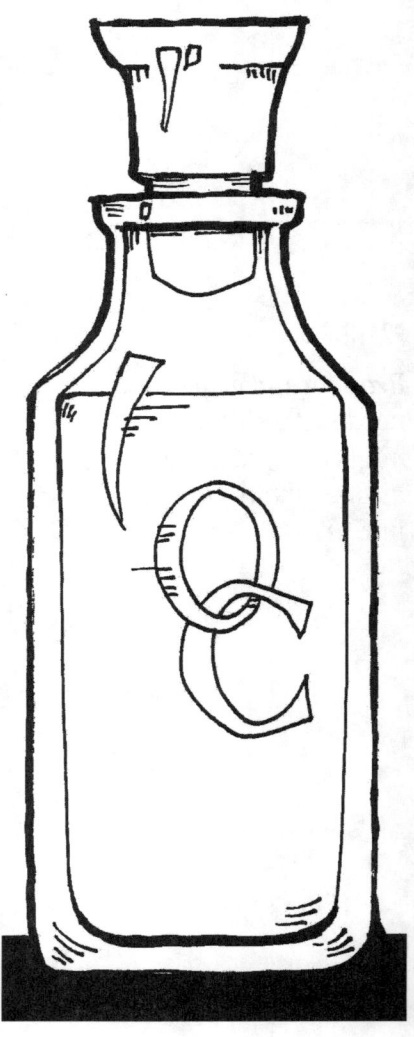

REFLECTING

What experiences of anointing do you remember? What happened when you were anointed? How did it make you feel?

30

REMEMBERING

We remember being anointed during the catechumenate with the oil of catechumens, oil meant to strengthen us for the journey and help us resist temptations to sin.

We remember being anointed with chrism after our baptism. Chrism is a scented oil that reminds us of "The Anointed One," Jesus the Christ. The priest or bishop told us that the anointing would make us "more like Christ" and would help us "to be witnesses to his suffering, death, and resurrection" and "active members of the Church" who "build up the Body of Christ in faith and love." The fragrance of this anointing with chrism lingered, reminding us and everyone around us that we had become the anointed of God.

REFLECTING

What did you experience as your were anointed with the oil of catechumens before your baptism? How did you feel? What effect did it have?

What did you experience as you were anointed with chrism just after your baptism—as you were confirmed? How did you feel? How can you be more like Christ; be a witness to his suffering, death, and resurrection; be an active member of the Church who builds up the Body of Christ in faith and love?

READING

Isaiah 61:1–11

> The spirit of the Lord God is upon me,
> > because the Lord has anointed me;
> He has sent me to bring glad tidings to the poor,
> > to heal the brokenhearted,
> To proclaim liberty to the captives
> > and release to the prisoners,
> To announce a year of favor from the Lord
> > and a day of vindication by our God,
> > to comfort all who mourn;
> To place on those who mourn in Zion
> > a diadem instead of ashes,
> To give them oil of gladness in place of mourning,
> > a glorious mantle instead of a listless spirit.
> They will be called oaks of justice,
> > planted by the Lord to show his glory.
>
> They shall rebuild the ancient ruins,
> > the former wastes they shall raise up
> And restore the ruined cities,
> > desolate now for generations.
> Strangers shall stand ready to pasture your flocks,
> > foreigners shall be your farmers and vinedressers.
> You yourselves shall be named priests of the Lord,
> > ministers of our God you shall be called.
> You shall eat the wealth of the nations
> > and boast of riches from them.
>
> Since their shame was double
> > and disgrace and spittle were their portion,
> They shall have a double inheritance in their land,
> > everlasting joy shall be theirs.
> For I, the Lord, love what is right,
> > I hate robbery and injustice;
> I will give them their recompense faithfully,
> > a lasting covenant I will make with them.
> Their descendants shall be renowned among the nations,
> > and their offspring among the peoples;
> All who see them shall acknowledge them
> > as a race the Lord has blessed.

> I rejoice heartily in the LORD,
> > in my God is the joy of my soul;
> For he has clothed me with a robe of salvation,
> > and wrapped me in a mantle of justice,
> Like a bridegroom adorned with a diadem,
> > like a bride bedecked with her jewels.
> As the earth brings forth its plants,
> > and a garden makes its growth spring up,
> So will the Lord GOD make justice and praise
> > spring up before all the nations.

Luke 4:16–21

He came to Nazareth, where he had grown up, and went according to his custom into the synagogue on the sabbath day. He stood up to read and was handed a scroll of the prophet Isaiah. He unrolled the scroll and found the passage where it was written:

> *The Spirit of the Lord is upon me,*
> > *because he has anointed me*
> > *to bring glad tidings to the poor.*
> *He has sent me to proclaim liberty to captives*
> > *and recovery of sight to the blind,*
> > *to let the oppressed go free,*
> > *and to proclaim a year acceptable to the Lord.*

Rolling up the scroll, he handed it back to the attendant and sat down, and the eyes of all in the synagogue looked intently at him. He said to them, "Today this Scripture passage is fulfilled in your hearing."

REFLECTING

Jesus was anointed "to bring glad tidings to the poor . . . to proclaim liberty to captives and recovery of sight to the blind, to let the oppressed go free, and to proclaim a year acceptable to the Lord." What have you been anointed to do?

The word "Christ" is derived from the Greek word for "the anointed one." Now that you are a "Christian," you are one of God's "anointed ones." How does that make you feel?

PRAYING

Take either Isaiah 61:1–2 or Luke 4:18–19 and pray these words yourself or write your own version indicating what you believe you have been anointed to do. In a group setting, pray one of these texts changing the word "me" to "us," or share the words you have written in a prayerful setting.

Isaiah 61:1–2
The spirit of the Lord God is upon me,
    because the Lord has anointed me;
He has sent me to bring glad tidings to the poor,
    to heal the brokenhearted,
To proclaim liberty to the captives
    and release to the prisoners,
To announce a year of favor from the Lord
    and a day of vindication by our God,
        to comfort all who mourn.

Luke 4:18–19
    The Spirit of the Lord is upon me,
        because he has anointed me
        to bring glad tidings to the poor.
    He has sent me to proclaim liberty to captives
        and recovery of sight to the blind,
        to let the oppressed go free,
    and to proclaim a year acceptable
        to the Lord.

Easter Friday

Place a plate with bread and a cup of wine in the center of the table. Use bread and wine, the paten and chalice generally used at Mass if available, as well as an assortment of fresh baked breads and a carafe or bottle of wine. Other items from earlier in the week might also be present.

REFLECTING

What foods and drinks have special memories for you? Are there any foods or drinks you cannot imagine living without?

REMEMBERING

We begin by remembering. We remember events long ago and not so long ago. We remember our favorite foods and drinks, those we asked for if a parent or grandparent asked us what we wanted to eat on a special occasion. We remember those foods and drinks that gave us comfort, that bring back happy memories of times past.

We remember that there are people today, just as there were people in the time of

Jesus, who could not imagine life without bread and wine. We live in a culture and place where a great variety of food and drink is available. Because of this no one food or drink carries that kind of weight for us. But there are people, like the poor of Guatemala, who could never imagine life without tortillas. There are people in our own culture who can't imagine a day that begins without a cup of coffee. When Jesus used bread and wine, he lived among people who could not imagine life without bread and wine.

READING

John 6:30–35

The crowd said to Jesus: "What sign can you do, that we may see and believe in you? What can you do? Our ancestors ate manna in the desert, as it is written:

He gave them bread from heaven to eat."

So Jesus said to them, "Amen, amen, I say to you, it was not Moses who gave the bread from heaven; my Father gives you the true bread from heaven. For the bread of God is that which comes down from heaven and gives life to the world."

So they said to him, "Sir, give us this bread always." Jesus said to them, "I am the bread of life; whoever comes to me will never hunger, and whoever believes in me will never thirst."

John 6:48–58

[Jesus said,] "I am the bread of life. Your ancestors ate the manna in the desert, but they died; this is the bread that comes down from heaven so that one may eat it and not die. I am the living bread that came down from heaven; whoever eats this bread will live forever; and the bread that I will give is my flesh for the life of the world."

The Jews quarreled among themselves, saying, "How can this man give us his flesh to eat?" Jesus said to them, "Amen, amen, I say to you, unless you eat the flesh of the Son of Man and drink his blood, you do not have life within you. Whoever eats my flesh and drinks my blood has eternal life, and I will raise him on the last day. For my flesh is true food, and my blood is true drink. Whoever eats my flesh and drinks my blood remains in me and I in him. Just as the living Father sent me and I have life because of the Father, so also the one who feeds on me will have life because of me. This is the bread that came down from heaven. Unlike your ancestors who ate and still died, whoever eats this bread will live forever."

REMEMBERING

Once, while visiting members of my religious community in Guatemala, I met a woman at Mass on Sunday morning. She was wet and covered with mud. She had fallen on the mountain trails while walking from her home to the parish church. She lived in one of almost fifty villages in the parish, where the priest only visits once or twice a year. She woke up as the sun was rising, and felt as if she would starve to death if she did not receive the Eucharist. She had not received Communion in three months, and was not likely to do so for the next three months. But that day, she was starving for the Body and Blood of Christ. So, she walked to church—walked for three hours through the mountains, knowing that it would take at least four hours to return home, as it is mostly uphill from the church to her village. Just as she could not imagine life without tortillas and beans, she could not imagine life without the Body and Blood of Christ.

REFLECTING

Most of us do not live in places where the Eucharist is not available. Most of us live in places where the Mass is celebrated at least weekly, if not daily. Many of us, as catechumens and as the elect, longed to receive the Eucharist. Some of us may have been starving as we longed for the day when we, too, would share the Body and Blood of Christ with others. What was it like to watch others receive Communion when you could not? What was your experience as you were dismissed, knowing that those left behind in the church would receive the Body and Blood of Christ, when you would not?

READING

Luke 24:13–35

That very day, the first day of the week, two of Jesus' disciples were going to a village seven miles from Jerusalem called Emmaus, and they were conversing about all the things that had occurred. And it happened that while they were conversing and debating, Jesus himself drew near and walked with them, but their eyes were prevented from recognizing him. He asked them, "What are you discussing as you walk along?" They stopped, looking downcast. One of them, named Cleopas, said to him in reply, "Are you the only visitor to Jerusalem who does not know of the things that have taken place there in these days?" And he replied to them, "What sort of things?" They said to him, "The things that happened to Jesus the Nazarene, who was a prophet mighty in deed and word before God and all the people, how our chief priests and rulers both handed him over to a sentence of death and crucified him. But we were hoping that he would be the one to redeem Israel; and besides all this, it is now the third day since this took place. Some women from our group, however, have astounded us: they were at the tomb early in the morning and did not find his body; they came back and reported that they had indeed seen a vision of angels who announced that he was alive. Then some of those with us went to the tomb and found things just as the women had described, but him they did not see." And he said to them, "Oh, how foolish you are! How slow of heart to believe all that the prophets spoke! Was it not necessary that the Christ should suffer these things and enter into his glory?" Then beginning with Moses and all the prophets, he interpreted to them what referred to him in all the Scriptures. As they approached the village to which they were going, he gave the impression that he was going on farther. But they urged him, "Stay with us, for it is nearly evening and the day is almost over." So he went in to stay with them. And it happened that, while he was with them at table, he took bread, said the blessing, broke it, and gave it to them. With that their eyes were opened and they recognized him, but he vanished from their sight. Then they said to each other, "Were not our hearts burning within us while he spoke to us on the way and opened the Scriptures to us?" So they set out at once and returned to Jerusalem where they found gathered together the eleven and those with them who were saying, "The Lord has truly been raised and has appeared to Simon!" Then the two recounted what had taken place on the way and how he was made known to them in the breaking of the bread.

REMEMBERING

They had only celebrated the breaking of the bread once before, at the Last Supper. Yet when he said the blessing, broke the bread, and gave it to them, they immediately recognized him. As they looked back on the encounter, they also recognized that their hearts had been burning within them as he shared the scriptures and interpreted those scriptures for them.

REFLECTING

Fully initiated in the Catholic Church only recently, you may have only celebrated the breaking of the bread once or twice. What has been your experience of celebrating the breaking of the bread? As you look back, what was your experience of having listened to the stories and heard them explained? Your journey may have been much longer than a walk from Jerusalem to Emmaus, but you have been on a faith journey. What were some of the highlights of that journey? When did your heart burn within you as you traveled toward the table where the Lord Jesus would share his body and blood with you?

READING

Read any one of the following:

Matthew 26:26–30

    While they were eating, Jesus took bread, said the blessing, broke it, and giving it to his disciples said, "Take and eat; this is my body." Then he took a cup, gave thanks, and gave it to them, saying, "Drink from it, all of you, for this is my blood of the covenant, which will be shed on behalf of many for the forgiveness of sins. I tell you, from now on I shall not drink this fruit of the vine until the day when I drink it with you new in the kingdom of my Father." Then, after singing a hymn, they went out to the Mount of Olives.

Mark 14:22–26

    While they were eating, he took bread, said the blessing, broke it, and gave it to them, and said, "Take it; this is my body." Then he took a cup, gave thanks, and gave it to them, and they all drank from it. He said to them, "This is my blood of the covenant, which will be shed for many. Amen, I say to you, I shall not drink again the fruit of the vine until the day when I drink it new in the kingdom of God." Then, after singing a hymn, they went out to the Mount of Olives.

Luke 22:14–20

    When the hour came, Jesus took his place at table with the apostles. He said to them, "I have eagerly desired to eat this Passover with you before I suffer, for, I tell you, I shall not eat it again until there is fulfillment in the kingdom of God." Then he took a cup, gave thanks, and said, "Take this and share it among yourselves; for I tell you that from this time on I shall not drink of the fruit of the vine until the kingdom of God comes." Then he took the bread, said the blessing, broke it, and gave it to them, saying, "This is my body, which will be given for you; do this in memory of me." And likewise the cup after they had eaten, saying, "This cup is the new covenant in my blood, which will be shed for you.

1 Corinthians 11:23–26

    Brothers and sisters: I received from the Lord what I also handed on to you, that the Lord Jesus, on the night he was handed over, took bread, and, after he had given thanks, broke it and said, "This is my body that is for you. Do this in remembrance of me." In the same way also the cup, after supper, saying, "This cup is the new covenant in my blood. Do this, as often as you drink it, in remembrance of me." For as often as you eat this bread and drink the cup, you proclaim the death of the Lord until he comes.

REFLECTING

Jesus said he would not share wine again until the kingdom of God had come. While the scriptures do not specifically speak of him sharing a cup of wine, they do tell us that he ate and drank with his disciples after the Resurrection. Does this mean that the kingdom of God has already come? If so, what difference does it make that we are living during the reign of God? How are you a witness to that reign? How do you imagine that eating and drinking in the reign of God at least every Sunday for the rest of your life will affect you?

PRAYING

Now would be an appropriate time to offer a prayer of thanksgiving for the gift of the Eucharist—for the breaking of the bread—for your sharing in the Body and Blood of Christ.

Easter Saturday

REMEMBERING

We begin by remembering. We remember events long ago and not so long ago. We may remember being sent to the store to pick up something forgotten or something we ran out of at the last minute. We might remember being sent to the principal's office to deliver a message or to be punished. We may remember being sent to get help for someone in an emergency or to find someone when a meal was ready to be served. We might remember being assigned to a menial task at work because we were the lowest person on the totem pole. We may remember being sent on a special mission to accomplish a particular task. We may remember being sent with fear and trepidation or with confidence and pride at being chosen for a great responsibility.

REFLECTING

Do you remember times of being sent when you knew exactly where you were going and what you were going to get or do? Do you remember times of being sent when you had no idea exactly what was expected of you? How did you feel in these different circumstances? How do you feel as you remember those events?

READING

Matthew 10:1–14

Jesus summoned his Twelve disciples and gave them authority over unclean spirits to drive them out and to cure every disease and every illness. The names of the Twelve Apostles are these: first, Simon called Peter, and his brother Andrew; James, the son of Zebedee, and his brother John; Philip and Bartholomew, Thomas and Matthew the tax collector; James, the son of Alphaeus, and Thaddeus; Simon the Cananean, and Judas Iscariot who betrayed Jesus.

Jesus sent out these Twelve after instructing them thus, "Do not go into pagan territory or enter a Samaritan town. Go rather to the lost sheep of the house of Israel. As you go, make this proclamation: 'The kingdom of heaven is at hand.' Cure the sick, raise the dead, cleanse lepers, drive out demons. Without cost you have received; without cost you are to give. Do not take gold or silver or copper for your belts; no sack for the journey, or a second tunic, or sandals, or walking stick. The laborer deserves his keep. Whatever town or village you enter, look for a worthy person in it, and stay there until you leave. As you enter a house, wish it peace. If the house is worthy, let your peace come upon it; if not, let your peace return to you. Whoever will not receive you or listen to your words—go outside that house or town and shake the dust from your feet.

or Luke 10:1–11

At that time the Lord appointed seventy-two others whom he sent ahead of him in pairs to every town and place he intended to visit. He said to them, "The harvest is abundant but the laborers are few; so ask the master of the harvest to send out laborers for his harvest. Go on your way; behold, I am sending you like lambs among wolves. Carry no money bag, no sack, no sandals; and greet no one along the way. Into whatever house you enter, first say, 'Peace to this household.' If a peaceful person lives there, your peace will rest on him; but if not, it will return to you. Stay in the same house and eat and drink what is offered to you, for the laborer deserves his payment. Do not move about from one house to another. Whatever town you enter and they welcome you, eat what is set before you, cure the sick in it and say to them, 'The kingdom of God is at hand for you.' Whatever town you enter and they do not receive you, go out into the streets and say, 'The dust of your town that clings to our feet, even that we shake off against you.' Yet know this: the kingdom of God is at hand.

REMEMBERING

Do you remember being sent to do something when you felt unprepared? The disciples must have felt unprepared at this time. Jesus had not yet finished instructing them. They had not yet witnessed all his miraculous powers. They had not yet heard all his parables. They had not yet celebrated the Last Supper or witnessed his death upon the cross. They had not known of the Resurrection or heard his final instructions. They were not ready for the mission on which he was sending them.

They hadn't figured out where they might be welcomed or where they might be rejected. They were sent not only to those who would listen, but also to those who would not. In Luke's account, they were told to respond with the same message regardless of how they were received. If received well, they were to tell the people, "The kingdom of God is at hand." If received poorly, they were to proclaim the same message: "The kingdom of God is at hand." Proclaiming the message seemed more important than whether or not anyone heard or responded to it.

Remember, too, that you are being sent, but you will never be sent alone. Jesus sent his disciples with nothing but each other. With someone else at their side they would have everything they needed to accomplish the mission on which they were sent.

REFLECTING

The early Christians had several names for what we do each Saturday evening or Sunday when we listen to the Word of God and share the Body and Blood of Christ. Sometimes it was simply called "The Breaking of the Bread." Other times it was called "Eucharist," the Greek word for thanksgiving. It was a thanksgiving feast—a time to give thanks to God for all God had done for them. But the name most commonly used throughout our history has been "Mass." It was given a name that described what it was all about—being sent. The Latin word from which we get the word "Mass" is missa, which means "sending." The early Christians experienced the Eucharist as the great sending. It was a time to come together in order to be sent to the world to proclaim that the reign of God is in our midst.

Each time we gather for Mass, we do so in order to be sent. How do you feel about being sent? You had only been fully initiated into the saving mysteries a few minutes and already the Church was sending you out. Ready or not, here you go! How did you witness to the resurrection during this past week? How often did what happened last Saturday evening come up in conversation this week? How did it affect what you said and did this week? Whether you knew it or not, you were sent!

READING

Matthew 28:16–20

The eleven disciples went to Galilee, to the mountain to which Jesus had ordered them. When they saw him, they worshiped, but they doubted. Then Jesus approached and said to them, "All power in heaven and on earth has been given to me. Go, therefore, and make disciples of all nations, baptizing them in the name of the Father, and of the Son, and of the holy Spirit, teaching them to observe all that I have commanded you. And behold, I am with you always, until the end of the age."

or Mark 16:15–20

Jesus said to his disciples, "Go into the whole world and proclaim the gospel to every creature. Whoever believes and is baptized will be saved; whoever does not believe will be condemned. These signs will accompany those who believe: in my name they will drive out demons, they will speak new languages. They will pick up serpents with their hands, and if they drink any deadly thing, it will not harm them. They will lay hands on the sick, and they will recover."

So then the Lord Jesus, after he spoke to them, was taken up into heaven and took his seat at the right hand of God. But they went forth and preached everywhere, while the Lord worked with them and confirmed the word through accompanying signs.

or Acts of the Apostles 1:3–8

He presented himself alive to them by many proofs after he had suffered, appearing to them during forty days and speaking about the kingdom of God. While meeting with them, he enjoined them not to depart from Jerusalem, but to wait for "the promise of the Father about which you have heard me speak; for John baptized with water, but in a few days you will be baptized with the Holy Spirit."

When they had gathered together they asked him, "Lord, are you at this time going to restore the kingdom to Israel?" He answered them, "It is not for you to know the times or seasons that the Father has established by his own authority. But you will receive power when the Holy Spirit comes upon you, and you will be my witnesses in Jerusalem, throughout Judea and Samaria, and to the ends of the earth."

REMEMBERING

In Matthew's Gospel, Jesus' final words are, "And behold, I am with you always, until the end of the age." We are not sent out alone. Even if our fellow believers do not go with us, we are not alone. The blood of Jesus flows through our veins. The body of Christ is part of who we are. The Spirit of God dwells in us and walks with us. We are never alone.

REFLECTING

How do you feel about that? Whether you feel Christ's presence in a profound way or not, Jesus walks with you! How does knowing that make you feel?

PRAYING

Take a few moments to rest in Christ's presence, to remember that you are in Christ and Christ is in you. Then tell the Lord whatever is on your mind. Give thanks or ask for whatever you need.

2nd Sunday of Easter

REMEMBERING

We begin by remembering. We remember events long ago and not so long ago. We remember how Jesus suddenly appeared to the disciples on the first Easter and how he offered them his peace.

We also remember times in our own lives when someone we didn't expect to be there suddenly appeared; when someone we hadn't seen in a long time, someone we never expected to see again, someone with whom we had once been close, suddenly reentered our lives. We might recall seeing someone for the first time after we had let them down, betrayed them, or turned our back on them. We remember how we felt when we first saw them. We may remember a time when we expected to be confronted by the one we disappointed, betrayed, abandoned, but instead were unexpectedly greeted warmly. We might recall a time when we felt abandoned, lost, or disillusioned, as if our world were falling apart, and suddenly the presence of a particular person changed everything. We may have experienced failure and suddenly a word, a phrase, or an encounter with another turned what seemed like failure into success.

REFLECTING

What were your feelings as those events occurred? How do you feel now as you recall such experiences?

These feelings must have been similar to those of the disciples when Jesus suddenly appeared to them shortly after they had witnessed his arrest, trial, and execution. They must have been afraid and then been overcome with joy.

READING

John 20:19–31

On the evening of that first day of the week, when the doors were locked, where the disciples were, for fear of the Jews, Jesus came and stood in their midst and said to them, "Peace be with you." When he had said this, he showed them his hands and his side. The disciples rejoiced when they saw the Lord. Jesus said to them again, "Peace be with you. As the Father has sent me, so I send you." And when he had said this, he breathed on them and said to them, "Receive the holy Spirit. Whose sins you forgive are forgiven them, and whose sins you retain are retained."

Thomas, called Didymus, one of the Twelve, was not with them when Jesus came. So the other disciples said to him, "We have seen the Lord." But he said to them, "Unless I see the mark of the nails in his hands and put my finger into the nailmarks and put my hand into his side, I will not believe."

Now a week later his disciples were again inside and Thomas was with them. Jesus came, although the doors were locked, and stood in their midst and said, "Peace be with you." Then he said to Thomas, "Put your finger here and see my hands, and bring your hand and put it into my side, and do not be unbelieving, but believe." Thomas answered and said to him, "My Lord and my God!" Jesus said to him, "Have you come to believe because you have seen me? Blessed are those who have not seen and have believed."

Now, Jesus did many other signs in the presence of his disciples that are not written in this book. But these are written that you may come to believe that Jesus is the Christ, the Son of God, and that through this belief you may have life in his name.

REMEMBERING

We may remember times when someone told a story too good to be true, when what they told us seemed just a bit too far-fetched. We may remember a time when someone told us something, but their words and their actions didn't seem to mesh. We may recall times when we doubted what someone else said, or when they doubted what we had told them.

Today, we remember what it must have been like when Thomas came back into the upper room. The other disciples told him that they had seen the Lord, that Jesus was risen from the dead. But the doors were still locked, the windows still shuttered. Their words were filled with excitement, but they were still gathered together in that locked upper room. They said one thing, but their actions seemed to indicate that they were still afraid, still unwilling to go out from that locked room to tell the world. And when Thomas doubted what they had to say, they just kept repeating the story as if saying it over and over again might make it true. Perhaps it was his fellow apostles whom Thomas doubted more than he doubted the story of Jesus' appearance.

REFLECTING

Mahatma Gandhi was once asked about Christianity. He said that our Christ was a great man, a holy man, but that Christians—those who claimed to be his followers—were the same people who were enslaving his people and the same people who had invented almost all of the great weapons used to destroy life. He said he could be a follower of Christ, but never a Christian.

The great historian G. K. Chesterton once wrote: "The Christian ideal has not been tried and found wanting; it has been found difficult and left untried."

Have there been times when your faith and your words about your faith didn't quite correspond with your actions? When have these discrepancies between words and actions caused others to doubt? When have discrepancies between the words and actions of others caused you to doubt?

REFLECTING

Perhaps Thomas doubted because his fellow disciples had "retained" his sins—had held back in forgiving him for his initial doubts. Perhaps that lack of forgiveness had only made his doubts grow stronger. Imagine what it might have been like. We can envision that Thomas was being bombarded with phrases like "You should have been here." These were phrases uttered not so much in joy as in accusation—experienced as condemnation rather than a sharing of the Good News. Have you ever encountered a Christian who used the gospel more as a weapon than as good news to be shared in joy and excitement?

REMEMBERING

In that upper room, Jesus says, "Peace be with you." He also says to his disciples, "Receive the Holy Spirit. Whose sins you forgive they are forgiven them, and whose sins you retain are retained." The scripture scholar Eugene LaVerdiere once said that the second sentence of the original text of this passage might be better translated, "If you do not forgive, they will never experience my mercy." One might phrase it as a question: "If you don't forgive, who will?"

REMEMBERING

We don't know much about what Saint Thomas did after the Ascension. There is very little written about what he did during the rest of his life. However, when the early Jesuit missionaries arrived in India in the fifteenth century, they were surprised to find a flourishing Christian church claiming Thomas as the one who had brought the message of the gospel to that part of the world. Apparently his response to his encounter with Christ was eventually to leave the upper room, to set off on a mission, to tell others the good news he had received.

REFLECTING

What does today's Gospel call you to do? How are you being challenged to witness your faith to others? How do you face your own doubts and the doubts of others—especially those who may wonder why anyone in their right mind would want to become a Catholic at this time in human history? How do you live in such a way that others might see an image of the Risen One in you?

PRAYING

You may want to ask Thomas to help you face your own doubts. You may want to ask him to pray with you as you implore God to help you be a witness of the Resurrection today.

3rd Sunday of Easter

REMEMBERING

We begin by remembering. We remember events long ago and not so long ago. We remember the surprise of meeting people we didn't expect to meet in a place we didn't expect to meet them. It may have been a joyful surprise or an embarrassing one. Perhaps we were walking along or standing in line or waiting or watching when suddenly we recognized someone we didn't expect to see at that particular time or place.

READING

Year A
Luke 24:1–35

At daybreak on the first day of the week the women who had come from Galilee with Jesus took the spices they had prepared and went to the tomb. They found the stone rolled away from the tomb; but when they entered, they did not find the body of the Lord Jesus. While they were puzzling over this, behold, two men in dazzling garments appeared to them. They were terrified and bowed their faces to the ground. They said to them, "Why do you seek the living one among the dead? He is not here, but he has been raised. Remember what he said to you while he was still in Galilee, that the Son of Man must be handed over to sinners and be crucified, and rise on the third day." And they remembered his words. Then they returned from the tomb and announced all these things to the eleven and to all the others. The women were Mary Magdalene, Joanna, and Mary the mother of James; the others who accompanied them also told this to the apostles, but their story seemed like nonsense and they did not believe them. But Peter got up and ran to the tomb, bent down, and saw the burial cloths alone; then he went home amazed at what had happened.

That very day, the first day of the week, two of Jesus' disciples were going to a village seven miles from Jerusalem called Emmaus, and they were conversing about all the things that had occurred. And it happened that while they were conversing and debating, Jesus himself drew near and walked with them, but their eyes were prevented from recognizing him. He asked them, "What are you discussing as you walk along?" They stopped, looking downcast. One of them, named Cleopas, said to him in reply, "Are you the only visitor to Jerusalem who does not know of the things that have taken place there in these days?" And he replied to them, "What sort of things?" They said to him, "The things that happened to Jesus the Nazarene, who was a prophet mighty in deed and word before God and all the people, how our chief priests and rulers both handed him over to a sentence of death and crucified him. But we were hoping that he would be the one to redeem Israel; and besides all this, it is now the third day since this took place. Some women from our group, however, have astounded us: they were at the tomb early in the morning and did not find his body; they came back and reported that they had indeed seen a vision of angels who announced that he was alive. Then some of those with us went to the tomb and found things just as the women had described, but him they did not see." And he said to them, "Oh, how foolish you are! How slow of heart to believe all that the prophets spoke! Was it not necessary that the Christ should suffer these things and enter into his glory?" Then beginning with Moses and all the prophets, he interpreted to them what referred to him in all the Scriptures. As they approached the village to which they were going, he gave the impression that he was going on farther. But they urged him, "Stay with us, for it is nearly evening and the day is almost over." So he went in to stay with them. And it happened that, while he was with them at table, he took bread, said the blessing, broke it, and gave it to them. With that their eyes were opened and they recognized him, but he vanished from their sight. Then they said to each other, "Were not our hearts burning within us while he spoke to us on the way and opened the Scriptures to us?" So they set out at once and returned to Jerusalem where they found gathered together the eleven and those with them who were saying, "The Lord has truly been raised and has appeared to Simon!" Then the two recounted what had taken place on the way and how he was made known to them in the breaking of the bread.

REFLECTING

Year A

Has anything like that ever happened in your life? Have you almost given up? Were you ever so discouraged by the way things were going that you decided just to go back to your old way of life? Has a stranger helped you to recognize things you didn't recognize yourself? Has that happened during the past year or so as you journeyed toward the Easter sacraments? Did you ever want to give up, turn back, or not recognize the truth?

Did you ever suddenly wonder why you never thought of it that way before? Did someone else say something that just made it all make sense?

Have you ever experienced God entering your life when you least expected it? What happened? How did that affect what was happening in your life? How did that affect the way you looked back at the past? How did that affect what you did from that time forward?

At the Easter Vigil, what was your experience during the breaking of the bread, when you received the Eucharist, the body and blood of Christ, for the first time? Did sharing the Eucharist change anything in your outlook?

Where else have you recognized the presence of the Lord? Have you wanted to tell others? Have you done so?

REMEMBERING
Year A

They had basically given up hope. They were not waiting around to see what would happen next. They were going to Emmaus, to sin city. Nothing had turned out the way they had expected, so they just gave up and headed away from everyone and everything in which they had placed their hope.

They were walking along, minding their own business, when suddenly, out of nowhere, a stranger appeared. He just walked up to them and joined in their conversation. He seemed friendly enough, so they didn't mind. But they must have been puzzled. He seemed to understand their experience better than they did. His explanation seemed to make sense out of the senseless. His questions were more insightful than their answers.

This stranger seemed to know more about what was going on than they did. And then suddenly, like a bolt out of the blue, they recognized who he was. This was no stranger after all! He was back! Their hope had returned in the breaking of the bread, in the sign he had given them just a few days before as they shared the Passover meal with him.

And so they had to return to Jerusalem. They just had to tell the others what happened!

READING

Year B

Luke 24:35–48

The two disciples recounted what had taken place on the way and how Jesus was made known to them in the breaking of the bread.

While they were still speaking about this, he stood in their midst and said to them, "Peace be with you." But they were startled and terrified and thought that they were seeing a ghost. Then he said to them, "Why are you troubled? And why do questions arise in your hearts? Look at my hands and my feet, that it is I myself. Touch me and see, because a ghost does not have flesh and bones as you can see I have." And as he said this, he showed them his hands and his feet. While they were still incredulous for joy and were amazed, he asked them, "Have you anything here to eat?" They gave him a piece of baked fish; he took it and ate it in front of them. He said to them, "These are my words that I spoke to you while I was still with you, that everything written about me in the law of Moses and in the prophets and psalms must be fulfilled." Then he opened their minds to understand the Scriptures. And he said to them, "Thus it is written that the Christ would suffer and rise from the dead on the third day and that repentance, for the forgiveness of sins, would be preached in his name to all the nations, beginning from Jerusalem. You are witnesses of these things."

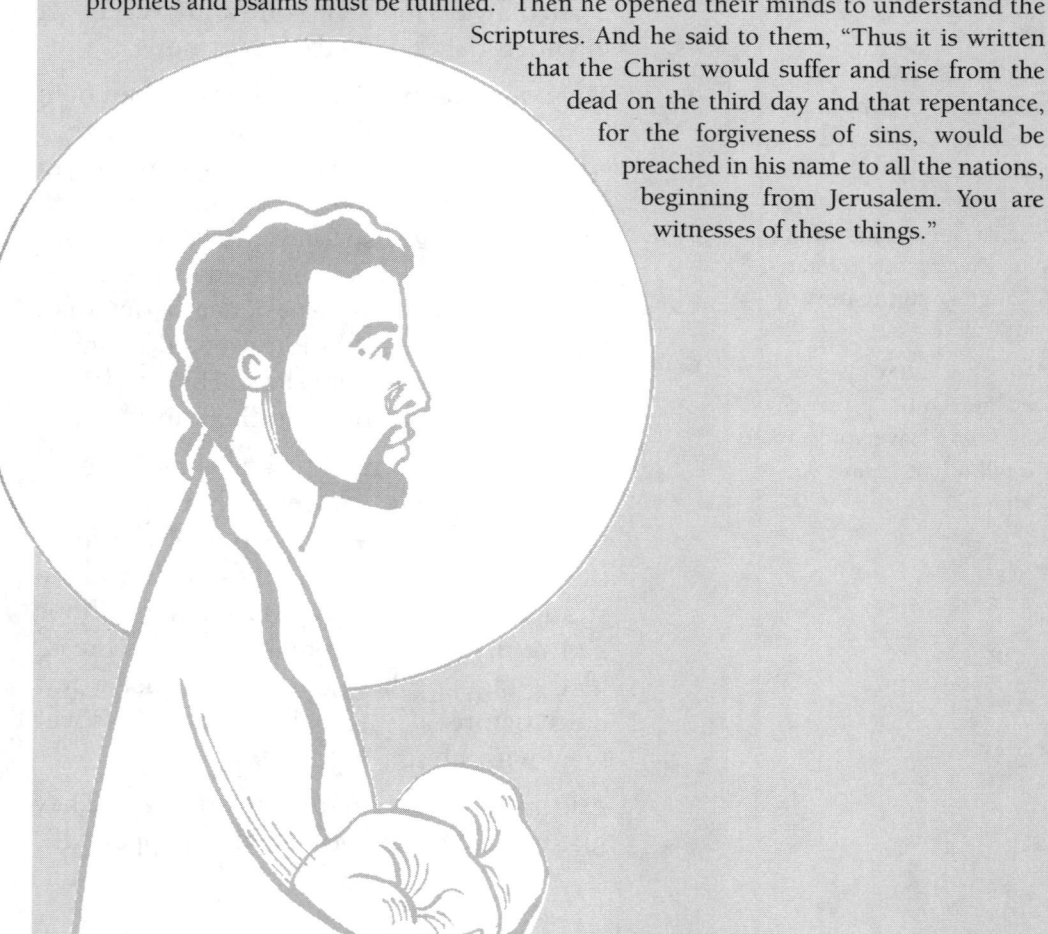

REFLECTING
Year B

Have you ever been surprised twice in the same day? While recounting an event, have you ever suddenly felt as if it were happening all over again, at that very moment? Have you felt the presence of God in such a way that you could almost touch that presence?

REMEMBERING
Year B

They had basically given up hope. They were not waiting around to see what would happen next. They were going to Emmaus, to sin city. Nothing had turned out the way they had expected, so they just gave up and headed away from everyone and everything in which they had placed their hope.

They were walking along, minding their own business, when suddenly, out of nowhere, a stranger appeared. He just walked up to them and joined in their conversation. He seemed friendly enough, so they didn't mind. But they must have been puzzled. He seemed to understand their experience better than they did. His explanation seemed to make sense out of the senseless. His questions were more insightful than their answers.

This stranger seemed to know more about what was going on than they did. And then suddenly, like a bolt out of the blue, they recognized who he was. This was no stranger after all! He was back! Their hope had returned in the breaking of the bread, in the sign he had given them just a few days before as they shared the Passover meal with him.

And so they had to return to Jerusalem. They just had to tell the others what happened! As they were telling the story of that encounter on the road to Emmaus, it happened again. Suddenly he was with them again. It was as if he appeared from nowhere. The doors had been locked, but somehow he got in. It was not their imagination. He was really there, eating and drinking, sharing with them all that he had shared with the two on the road to Emmaus.

READING

Year C
John 21:1–19

At that time, Jesus revealed himself again to his disciples at the Sea of Tiberias. He revealed himself in this way. Together were Simon Peter, Thomas called Didymus, Nathanael from Cana in Galilee, Zebedee's sons, and two others of his disciples. Simon Peter said to them, "I am going fishing." They said to him, "We also will come with you." So they went out and got into the boat, but that night they caught nothing. When it was already dawn, Jesus was standing on the shore; but the disciples did not realize that it was Jesus. Jesus said to them, "Children, have you caught anything to eat?" They answered him, "No." So he said to them, "Cast the net over the right side of the boat and you will find something." So they cast it, and were not able to pull it in because of the number of fish. So the disciple whom Jesus loved said to Peter, "It is the Lord." When Simon Peter heard that it was the Lord, he tucked in his garment, for he was lightly clad, and jumped into the sea. The other disciples came in the boat, for they were not far from shore, only about a hundred yards, dragging the net with the fish. When they climbed out on shore, they saw a charcoal fire with fish on it and bread. Jesus said to them, "Bring some of the fish you just caught." So Simon Peter went over and dragged the net ashore full of one hundred fifty-three large fish. Even though there were so many, the net was not torn. Jesus said to them, "Come, have breakfast." And none of the disciples dared to ask him, "Who are you?" because they realized it was the Lord. Jesus came over and took the bread and gave it to them, and in like manner the fish. This was now the third time Jesus was revealed to his disciples after being raised from the dead.

When they had finished breakfast, Jesus said to Simon Peter, "Simon, son of John, do you love me more than these?" Simon Peter answered him, "Yes, Lord, you know that I love you." Jesus said to him, "Feed my lambs." He then said to Simon Peter a second time, "Simon, son of John, do you love me?" Simon Peter answered him, "Yes, Lord, you know that I love you." Jesus said to him, "Tend my sheep." Jesus said to him the third time, "Simon, son of John, do you love me?" Peter was distressed that Jesus had said to him a third time, "Do you love me?" and he said to him, "Lord, you know everything; you know that I love you." Jesus said to him, "Feed my sheep. Amen, amen, I say to you, when you were younger, you used to dress yourself and go where you wanted; but when you grow old, you will stretch out your hands, and someone else will dress you and lead you where you do not want to go." He said this signifying by what kind of death he would glorify God. And when he had said this, he said to him, "Follow me."

REFLECTING
Year C

Have you ever tried to walk away from something—from a relationship, from a responsibility, from a direction your life was taking that you weren't sure you wanted to take? Have you ever experienced that *déjà vu*, that sense of "I've been here before" or "It's happening all over again"?

Have you ever had an experience of someone showing up when you least expected it, when you were embarrassed because you got caught doing something you had indicated you'd never do again? Have you expected to be reprimanded for doing something, only to have the one who had every right to be upset or angry react with generosity and compassion?

Have you ever betrayed someone and been forgiven? Have you ever betrayed a trust only to be trusted with more? Remember that Peter denied the Lord, but each time he said he loved him, Jesus called him to greater responsibility—"Feed my lambs, tend my sheep."

REMEMBERING
Year C

They had gone back to their old way of life—fishermen once again. And they didn't seem to be very good at it; once again they caught nothing all night. It had been a long night, and they were discouraged. First, the one for whom they had given up fishing in the first place had been condemned by both the religious and political leaders of their day. He whom they had come to believe would save Israel from all its problems was humiliated and executed like the most vicious criminals of that time and place. He for whom they had given up everything had gone somewhere no one wanted to follow—to the cross and beyond.

They had heard the woman's testimony. They had seen him themselves behind the locked doors and shuttered windows of the upper room. But it all seemed so unreal. The dead do not come back to life. Even though they had seen him, they still went back to their old way of life.

Then suddenly it happened again, just as it had happened so very long ago. A stranger on the beach suggested they throw their nets on the other side of the boat. The size of the catch was astounding. They must have remembered the first time he did that. He was really there, on the beach, doing it again: calling them back to who they had become, to the life they had lived. They were walking away from discipleship and he was calling them back once again.

PRAYING

Offer a prayer of thanksgiving, remembering Christ's compassion and mercy in your life.

MORE REFLECTING
All Years

God sometimes surprises us. Have you been surprised recently? Have you been tempted to go back to the way things were before you were fully initiated into the mystery of Christ? Have you been tempted to walk away from this new way of living? Have you experienced God's mercy? Have you experienced God's real presence in your life?

Imagine being there—on the road, in the upper room, or on the lake. Imagine him talking to you, sharing with you. Whatever doubts you may have, whatever failures have been a part of your life, remember them. And remember that he is with you now. What does he have to say? How does he offer you the same hope, the same mercy he showed the disciples so long ago?

4th Sunday of Easter

REMEMBERING
Year A

We begin by remembering. We remember events long ago and not so long ago. We remember situations when we have felt left out, abandoned, or forgotten. We may have literally been locked out, not welcomed, uninvited, or not allowed in where others have been let in. We may have been barred, for one reason or another, from a place we've wanted to go.

We've also experienced what it is like to be welcomed into a place we've never been before. We've been invited or taken to places we've wanted to see or experience. We might have gone to places we had longed to see. We may have been made welcome by strangers or people we barely knew. It might have been the first time we were invited to sit with the adults instead of the children at some family event, or the first time we set foot in some really spectacular place, someplace we weren't sure if we really belonged.

We may have experienced being led into places where we've felt safe or into places where our safety has been threatened. In certain places we feel at home. In other places we feel like strangers, as if we shouldn't be there or are not welcome or somehow don't deserve to be there.

When and where have you experienced being welcomed into a place where you felt safe enough to share your deepest self?

READING
Year A

John 10:1–10

Jesus said, "Amen, amen, I say to you, whoever does not enter a sheepfold through the gate but climbs over elsewhere is a thief and a robber. But whoever enters through the gate is the shepherd of the sheep. The gatekeeper opens it for him, and the sheep hear his voice, as he calls his own sheep by name and leads them out. When he has driven out all his own, he walks ahead of them, and the sheep follow him, because they recognize his voice. But they will not follow a stranger; they will run away from him, because they do not recognize the voice of strangers." Although Jesus used this figure of speech, the Pharisees did not realize what he was trying to tell them.

So Jesus said again, "Amen, amen, I say to you, I am the gate for the sheep. All who came before me are thieves and robbers, but the sheep did not listen to them. I am the gate. Whoever enters through me will be saved, and will come in and go out and find pasture. A thief comes only to steal and slaughter and destroy; I came so that they might have life and have it more abundantly."

REFLECTING
Year A

How have you experienced the Church as a safe place? How have you experienced your initiation into the Church as a gate that leads you to a place where it is safe enough to be yourself, to share your deepest feelings, to open your heart to God and others? How has Christ been a gate to new experiences in your life? Who have been some of the people who opened the way for you, who made you feel safe and secure, who introduced you to the ways of faith?

REMEMBERING
Year B & C

We begin by remembering. We remember events long ago and not so long ago. We remember being shepherded. Though we've probably never met a shepherd or even met someone who's met one, we have experienced being shepherded. We've been led like sheep—just part of the crowd. It may have been when we were students on the playground, lined up during a fire drill, or after recess. It may have been on a field trip or at an amusement park. Most of us, at one time or another, have been led as part of a group from one place to another. It may have been for our own safety, or it may have been for the safety of others or of precious objects. We may have felt protected or as if we were a danger to someone else or as if we weren't trusted.

We've probably all felt like part of the herd at one time or another. It may have been while waiting in an especially long line. We may have experienced being a number rather than a person. But on rare occasions, being herded in just the right way may actually have saved us. It may not have happened to us, but it did happen to those thousands of people who were evacuated from the World Trade Center on September 11, 2001. They were led by someone else to the safest stairway, to their own safety. They were shepherded to safety. Some were saved by shepherds who went into the buildings, looking for those who were lost, and many of them not only risked their lives, but died trying to shepherd strangers to safety.

Do you remember any other similar event, possibly even in your own life?

READING
Year B

John 10:11–18

Jesus said, "I am the good shepherd. A good shepherd lays down his life for the sheep. A hired man, who is not a shepherd and whose sheep are not his own, sees a wolf coming and leaves the sheep and runs away, and the wolf catches and scatters them. This is because he works for pay and has no concern for the sheep. I am the good shepherd, and I know mine and mine know me, just as the Father knows me and I know the Father; and I will lay down my life for the sheep. I have other sheep that do not belong to this fold. These also I must lead, and they will hear my voice, and there will be one flock, one shepherd. This is why the Father loves me, because I lay down my life in order to take it up again. No one takes it from me, but I lay it down on my own. I have power to lay it down, and power to take it up again. This command I have received from my Father."

READING
Year C

John 10:27–30

Jesus said: "My sheep hear my voice; I know them, and they follow me. I give them eternal life, and they shall never perish. No one can take them out of my hand. My Father, who has given them to me, is greater than all, and no one can take them out of the Father's hand. The Father and I are one."

REFLECTING
Years B & C

What kind of experiences of being shepherded have you had? What did they feel like? Who were the shepherds and what were their motivations? Did what they did comfort you, save you, or make things easier for you and for others? How did it feel? How have you felt shepherded as you explored your faith and came to full initiation in the Church?

Have you ever shepherded others? Have you guided someone else to safety?

READING
Years A, B, & C

John 21:15–17

When they had finished breakfast, Jesus said to Simon Peter, "Simon, son of John, do you love me more than these?" Simon Peter answered him, "Yes, Lord, you know that I love you." Jesus said to him, "Feed my lambs." He then said to Simon Peter a second time, "Simon, son of John, do you love me?" Simon Peter answered him, "Yes, Lord, you know that I love you." Jesus said to him, "Tend my sheep." Jesus said to him the third time, "Simon, son of John, do you love me?" Peter was distressed that Jesus had said to him a third time, "Do you love me?" and he said to him, "Lord, you know everything; you know that I love you." Jesus said to him, "Feed my sheep."

READING
Years A, B, & C

Matthew 25:31–46

Jesus said to his disciples: "When the Son of Man comes in his glory, and all the angels with him, he will sit upon his glorious throne, and all the nations will be assembled before him. And he will separate them one from another, as a shepherd separates the sheep from the goats. He will place the sheep on his right and the goats on his left. Then the king will say to those on his right, 'Come, you who are blessed by my Father. Inherit the kingdom prepared for you from the foundation of the world. For I was hungry and you gave me food, I was thirsty and you gave me drink, a stranger and you welcomed me, naked and you clothed me, ill and you cared for me, in prison and you visited me.' Then the righteous will answer him and say, 'Lord, when did we see you hungry and feed you, or thirsty and give you drink? When did we see you a stranger and welcome you, or naked and clothe you? When did we see you ill or in prison, and visit you?' And the king will say to them in reply, 'Amen, I say to you, whatever you did for one of these least brothers of mine, you did for me.' Then he will say to those on his left, 'Depart from me, you accursed, into the eternal fire prepared for the devil and his angels. For I was hungry and you gave me no food, I was thirsty and you gave me no drink, a stranger and you gave me no welcome, naked and you gave me no clothing, ill and in prison, and you did not care for me.' Then they will answer and say, 'Lord, when did we see you hungry or thirsty or a stranger or naked or ill or in prison, and not minister to your needs?' He will answer them, 'Amen, I say to you, what you did not do for one of these least ones, you did not do for me.' And these will go off to eternal punishment, but the righteous to eternal life."

PRAYING

Spend a few minutes in prayer giving thanks to God for those who have shepherded you and for the ways in which God has shepherded you throughout your life.

Ask God for the graces you need to discover the ways you can be a shepherd for others.

REFLECTING
Years A, B, & C

Have you heard the call to "feed my lambs . . . tend my sheep"? What has been your response to the call issued in these words: "Whatever you did for one of my least brothers [or sisters] of mine, you did for me"?

5th Sunday of Easter
Year A

REMEMBERING

We begin by remembering. We remember events long ago and not so long ago. We remember farewells—times when others have left us for one reason or another, when someone we cared for or who cared for us moved, changed schools or jobs. We remember times when we've been the ones who've moved on. We remember saying good-bye to friends and family members. We may remember ending a relationship or breaking up with a boyfriend or girlfriend. We might remember when someone we loved went off to college, to war, to a new job, to a new family, or to a distant place. Sometimes we weren't sure if we'd ever see them again.

We may even remember some final farewells. Perhaps we sat at the bedside of someone who was dying or stood or knelt before that person's body after death. We recall final words and sentiments. We remember the feelings, the loneliness, the joy of memories past, and the pain of knowing that they would not be part of any future memories.

Today's Gospel is a farewell message from Jesus to his disciples. But they aren't sure where he is going or why he is leaving. They don't quite understand the significance of his words.

READING

John 14:1–12

Jesus said to his disciples: "Do not let your hearts be troubled. You have faith in God; have faith also in me. In my Father's house there are many dwelling places. If there were not, would I have told you that I am going to prepare a place for you? And if I go and prepare a place for you, I will come back again and take you to myself, so that where I am you also may be. Where I am going you know the way." Thomas said to him, "Master, we do not know where you are going; how can we know the way?" Jesus said to him, "I am the way and the truth and the life. No one comes to the Father except through me. If you know me, then you will also know my Father. From now on you do know him and have seen him." Philip said to him, "Master, show us the Father, and that will be enough for us." Jesus said to him, "Have I been with you for so long a time and you still do not know me, Philip? Whoever has seen me has seen the Father. How can you say, 'Show us the Father'? Do you not believe that I am in the Father and the Father is in me? The words that I speak to you I do not speak on my own. The Father who dwells in me is doing his works. Believe me that I am in the Father and the Father is in me, or else, believe because of the works themselves. Amen, amen, I say to you, whoever believes in me will do the works that I do, and will do greater ones than these, because I am going to the Father."

REFLECTING

Now that you've been a fully initiated Catholic Christian for just over four weeks, how have things changed in your life? Has the excitement of the Easter Vigil begun to die down? Do you miss the time spent together with other catechumens after the Sunday dismissal? Are there things you wish you knew more about?

Like Philip, do you still have questions you want to ask—questions you need to ask before ending this phase of the initiation process? Are there things you heard about or witnessed, but want to know more about as you continue to live the Christian life?

REMEMBERING

The disciples were afraid. They didn't know where Jesus was going or why he was going. They didn't want him to leave. They wanted him to be with them forever—or at least for the rest of their lives. They had heard everything he said, but still they didn't understand. He had shown them the Father, but they still had not seen.

PRAYING

Ask God to help you continue to seek answers to your questions of faith.

5th Sunday of Easter — Year B

REMEMBERING

We begin by remembering. We remember events long ago and not so long ago. We remember the stories we heard as children, stories in which things weren't exactly what they seemed to be. We remember stories in which animals talked, trees acted, or people had magical powers. We remember stories that touch our hearts. It didn't matter that they weren't true stories, because they were stories that somehow contained the truth.

Perhaps there really wasn't a Cinderella, but a story in which a good, simple young woman triumphs when all the odds seemed against her gives us hope. Perhaps there is no land of Oz, but the wisdom of the Scarecrow, the love of the Tin Man and the courage of the Cowardly Lion inspire us still. Stories have a way of touching our hearts.

Today Jesus uses an image from creation. He tells a story. We are not really branches, and he is not really a vine. But somehow his story touches us, reminds us of how close we really are to him and to one another. Jesus gives us hope and courage as we face the challenges of life.

READING

John 15:1–8

Jesus said to his disciples: "I am the true vine, and my Father is the vine grower. He takes away every branch in me that does not bear fruit, and everyone that does he prunes so that it bears more fruit. You are already pruned because of the word that I spoke to you. Remain in me, as I remain in you. Just as a branch cannot bear fruit on its own unless it remains on the vine, so neither can you unless you remain in me. I am the vine, you are the branches. Whoever remains in me and I in him will bear much fruit, because without me you can do nothing. Anyone who does not remain in me will be thrown out like a branch and wither; people will gather them and throw them into a fire and they will be burned. If you remain in me and my words remain in you, ask for whatever you want and it will be done for you. By this is my Father glorified, that you bear much fruit and become my disciples."

REMEMBERING

The same sap that runs through the vine runs through the branches. The same sap that runs through one branch runs through all the branches. The same life source that nourishes the vine nourishes its branches. The branch may not have direct contact with the ground, with the water, or the nutrients within the earth, but the branch has life because the vine has that contact.

The same precious blood that runs through Jesus' veins and arteries runs through my veins and arteries, runs through your veins and arteries, runs through the veins and arteries of every person saved by the one who calls himself "the true vine." I may not have direct contact with God, but I share in the same life, the same nourishment, the same grace that is Christ—and so do you, as do all those united with Christ.

PRAYING

Give thanks to God that some of the precious blood of Christ runs through your veins and arteries. Ask God to help you recognize the divine in both yourself and others whom you encounter this week.

REFLECTING

How have you experienced Christ's divine life, his divine "sap", running through your veins and arteries? Have there been people you've encountered who obviously are filled with that divine sap? What is it about them that makes you think that?

How do you feel knowing that that same divine sap runs through you? Divinity runs through your veins and arteries! What challenges does that present for you and the way you live?

That same divine sap runs in everyone you meet, even in those you will never meet. What difference does that make? How might that affect the way you relate to them? If both you and someone else have the same divine sap within, how can you be enemies?

5th Sunday of Easter
Year C

REMEMBERING

We begin by remembering. We remember events long ago and not so long ago. We remember experiences of betrayal, perhaps when we were children. A brother or sister, a friend or classmate pointed a finger in our direction after a parent, teacher, or other adult asked, "Who did that?" Someone may have betrayed a confidence, broken a promise, taken someone else's side in an argument. At one time or another, in small things and in larger events, we may have felt the pain of betrayal.

We also remember farewells—times when others have left us for one reason or another, when someone we cared for or who cared for us moved, changed schools or jobs. We remember times when we've been the ones who've moved on. We remember saying good-bye to friends and family members. We may remember ending a relationship, breaking up with a boyfriend or girlfriend. We might remember when someone we loved went off to college, to war, to a new job, to a new family, or to a distant place. We weren't sure if we'd ever see them again.

We may even remember some final farewells. Perhaps we sat at the bedside of someone who was dying or stood or knelt before that person's body after death. We recall final words and sentiments. We remember the feelings, the loneliness, the joy of memories past, and the pain of knowing that they would not be part of any future memories.

Today's Gospel speaks of both betrayals and farewells. In both circumstances, Jesus responds positively to what we would normally consider negative experiences. We might also remember times of betrayal and farewell that, when we look back at them from some distance, in fact led us to where we are today. When one relationship ended we moved on and perhaps discovered a new relationship that has been more of a blessing than we could ever have imagined. One farewell opened doors to a new experience we otherwise would never have had.

REMEMBERING

It was a celebration of Passover, usually a time of great joy for the people of Israel. Yet Jesus was saying good-bye. It was a time of remembering how God had triumphed. Yet it looked as if he was about to be defeated. It was a time to remember blessings. Yet it looked as if they and their master might be cursed. Rumors were rampant. Enemies were launching plans. One of them was about to betray him. Yet Jesus speaks of being glorified.

He had just washed their feet, the Master treating his disciples as masters. He had already told them that they should do as he had done. He had already pointed out that one of them would betray him—and they all watched as Judas departed. They knew what could happen, and must have wondered what would happen to them.

The end may be near. Yet he is still instructing them on how to be his disciples. He gives them a new commandment: love one another. Once he is arrested, once he is condemned, once he is executed, it is a commandment they will need to remember.

READING

John 13:31–33a, 34–35

When Judas had left them, Jesus said, "Now is the Son of Man glorified, and God is glorified in him. If God is glorified in him, God will also glorify him in himself, and he will glorify him at once. My children, I will be with you only a little while longer. I give you a new commandment: love one another. As I have loved you, so you also should love one another. This is how all will know that you are my disciples, if you have love for one another."

READING

Acts 14:21–27

After Paul and Barnabas had proclaimed the good news to that city and made a considerable number of disciples, they returned to Lystra and to Iconium and to Antioch. They strengthened the spirits of the disciples and exhorted them to persevere in the faith, saying, "It is necessary for us to undergo many hardships to enter the kingdom of God." They appointed presbyters for them in each church and, with prayer and fasting, commended them to the Lord in whom they had put their faith. Then they traveled through Pisidia and reached Pamphylia. After proclaiming the word at Perga they went down to Attalia. From there they sailed to Antioch, where they had been commended to the grace of God for the work they had now accomplished. And when they arrived, they called the church together and reported what God had done with them and how he had opened the door of faith to the Gentiles.

REFLECTING

It is four weeks now since the excitement of the Easter Vigil. The patterns of everyday life have returned. There may already have been some days of disappointment, times of turmoil, feelings of futility—at home, at work, or while out and about. How did you respond? Was it distinct from the way you would have responded to a similar situation in the past? Do you wish your response had been different?

REMEMBERING

Paul had been treated like a god in Lystra, and then, just a short time later, betrayed, stoned, and dragged out of the city. He had gone on to preach in Derbe, and there he reminded the Christian community that they, too, would "undergo many hardships." And when he returned home to Antioch, he didn't whine about how he had been treated or the hardships he had endured. Instead, he "reported what God had done with them and how God had opened the door of faith to the Gentiles."

REFLECTING

Paul and Jesus offer us parting words today: "Love one another" and "It is necessary to undergo many hardships to enter the kingdom of God."

How do their farewell admonitions challenge you as you face the difficulties of life? Where did they find the strength to face the betrayals, denials, sufferings, and hardships of life? Where do you or could you find such strength?

If you knew you were about to die, what parting words would you have for those who love you? What words of wisdom would you want to share with them?

Love One Another as I have Loved You.

PRAYING

Place any hardships you are currently experiencing into the hands of God, and ask God for the grace you need to love others in these situations.

6th Sunday of Easter
Years A & C

REMEMBERING

We begin by remembering. We remember events long ago and not so long ago. We remember promises made and promises kept. We also remember promises made and promises broken. We remember promises made *to* us and promises made *by* us. We may remember promises made as someone was leaving, even if only for a little while. As children, we remember promises made by parents who left us with a babysitter, a neighbor, relative, or friend: "Don't worry, I'll be back." We might also remember the admonition that followed: "Be good until I get back."

Sometimes these promises were comforting. Sometimes they were not. Sometimes they gave us hope that the one who made the promise would not be gone for long. Sometimes, in spite of promises to the contrary, relationships have faded and ended as promises to keep in touch were not kept. Sometimes, however, even though time and space have kept us apart from someone we cared about, that relationship has continued, may even have grown.

READING

Year A

John 14:15–21

Jesus said to his disciples: "If you love me, you will keep my commandments. And I will ask the Father, and he will give you another Advocate to be with you always, the Spirit of truth, whom the world cannot accept, because it neither sees nor knows him. But you know him, because he remains with you, and will be in you. I will not leave you orphans; I will come to you. In a little while the world will no longer see me, but you will see me, because I live and you will live. On that day you will realize that I am in my Father and you are in me and I in you. Whoever has my commandments and observes them is the one who loves me. And whoever loves me will be loved by my Father, and I will love him and reveal myself to him."

Year C

John 14:23–29

Jesus said to his disciples: "Whoever loves me will keep my word, and my Father will love him, and we will come to him and make our dwelling with him. Whoever does not love me does not keep my words; yet the word you hear is not mine but that of the Father who sent me.

"I have told you this while I am with you. The Advocate, the Holy Spirit that the Father will send in my name, will teach you everything and remind you of all that I told you. Peace I leave with you; my peace I give to you. Not as the world gives do I give it to you. Do not let your hearts be troubled or afraid. You heard me tell you, 'I am going away and I will come back to you.' If you loved me, you would rejoice that I am going to the Father; for the Father is greater than I. And now I have told you this before it happens, so that when it happens you may believe."

REMEMBERING

He had recently washed their feet, given them a new commandment, to love one another, and had warned them about betrayals and denials. He told them that he would soon be leaving. He told them where he was going and that they could not come with him. Then he spoke to them of the Advocate who would be with them always—"the Spirit of truth . . . the Holy Spirit that the Father [would send] in his name." He spoke to them of their love for him and his love for them. He sought to reassure them just before he was arrested and taken away, crucified, killed, and buried. No matter what it might look like he wanted them to know that they would not be alone, that he would be coming back.

The disciples were not sure what would happen next. Jesus knew what would follow. We, too, know what happened next—and what happened after that. We know what happened later that night, the next day on Calvary, and even over the days and weeks that followed—at the empty tomb, along the road to Emmaus, in the upper room, on the shores of the sea of Galilee. We know about his death and his resurrection. We know that he appeared to them and that they received the Holy Spirit.

Even knowing all of that, we still sometimes feel left alone, abandoned, afraid, and discouraged. We still sometimes wonder when we'll recognize God at work in our lives again.

Take a moment to look back at all that has happened over the past months—or even years—as you journeyed toward the Easter sacraments and full membership in the Church. Were there moments when you were absolutely certain that you were in the presence of the Lord? Were there moments when you experienced God's grace at work in your life? Were there times when you felt sad, as the disciples must have as they heard the Lord speak about his departure from them? How did you keep hope alive?

Did you experience an Advocate who gave you hope?

READING

Year A

1 Peter 3:15–18

Beloved: Sanctify Christ as Lord in your hearts. Always be ready to give an explanation to anyone who asks you for a reason for your hope, but do it with gentleness and reverence, keeping your conscience clear, so that, when you are maligned, those who defame your good conduct in Christ may themselves be put to shame. For it is better to suffer for doing good, if that be the will of God, than for doing evil. For Christ also suffered for sins once, the righteous for the sake of the unrighteous, that he might lead you to God. Put to death in the flesh, he was brought to life in the Spirit.

Year C

Revelation 21:10–14, 22–23

The angel took me in spirit to a great, high mountain and showed me the holy city Jerusalem coming down out of heaven from God. It gleamed with the splendor of God. Its radiance was like that of a precious stone, like jasper, clear as crystal. It had a massive, high wall, with twelve gates where twelve angels were stationed and on which names were inscribed, the names of the twelve tribes of the Israelites. There were three gates facing east, three north, three south, and three west. The wall of the city had twelve courses of stones as its foundation, on which were inscribed the twelve names of the twelve apostles of the Lamb.

I saw no temple in the city, for its temple is the Lord God almighty and the Lamb. The city had no need of sun or moon to shine on it, for the glory of God gave it light, and its lamp was the Lamb.

REFLECTING

Year A
Are you "ready to give an explanation to anyone who asks you for a reason for your hope"?

Year C
Does John's vision give you hope? How do you imagine paradise? How would you describe heaven?

PRAYING

Spend a few moments thanking God for past blessings. Ask God to help you be hopeful throughout life. Ask Christ to help you remember that he is with you always and that you have already been blessed by the Spirit's gifts. Bring to the Lord any situations in your life or in the world that appear hopeless. Place them in God's hands.

6th Sunday of Easter
Year B

REMEMBERING

We begin by remembering. We remember events long ago and not so long ago. We remember final farewells. We might remember the words of someone we loved as they prepared for death, a friend who was moving away, or a coworker who was taking another job. We may remember commencement speeches, messages written in yearbooks, final instructions from someone who was turning over some responsibilities to us. We may recall words of wisdom shared as we set off on a new adventure, prepared to walk down the aisle, or stepped into a new future. Some of these words may be encouraging, some filled with warning, some filled with excitement, others with foreboding.

We might also remember words that at the time we did not realize would be the last words we would hear from a particular person. We may cherish these words or wish we could forget them. Some final words have a way of staying with us for the long haul.

READING

John 15:9–17

Jesus said to his disciples: "As the Father loves me, so I also love you. Remain in my love. If you keep my commandments, you will remain in my love, just as I have kept my Father's commandments and remain in his love.

"I have told you this so that my joy may be in you and your joy may be complete. This is my commandment: love one another as I love you. No one has greater love than this, to lay down one's life for one's friends. You are my friends if you do what I command you. I no longer call you slaves, because a slave does not know what his master is doing. I have called you friends, because I have told you everything I have heard from my Father. It was not you who chose me, but I who chose you and appointed you to go and bear fruit that will remain, so that whatever you ask the Father in my name he may give you. This I command you: love one another."

REMEMBERING

They were all gathered in the upper room to celebrate the holiest day of the year—the day when Israel remembered how God had led the people from slavery to freedom, from despair to hope, from Egypt to the Promised Land. The Master went down on his hands and knees and washed their feet. He talked to them of betrayal and denial, of his own departure, and the promise of an Advocate who would be with them always. They had heard the story of the vine and the branches, and now he was commanding them once again to love one another. Though a cloud of uncertainty and fear may have hovered over the room, the Master spoke of love. He reminded them of how they had come together: loved and loving, gathered that their "joy might be complete," more than disciples—friends—chosen and appointed "to go and bear fruit."

The evangelists wrote down the early church's memories of Jesus' farewell instructions to his disciples. The memories themselves have inspired countless others who were not present. They have given hope to others who were facing betrayal, denial, or feelings of abandonment.

REFLECTING

It's been a little more than a month since we celebrated our own Passover. We commemorated Jesus' passing over from death to new life and our own passing through the waters of baptism to new life as a Catholic Christian. What memories do you have of that night? What words do you remember?

Jesus told those gathered that he no longer called them slaves, but friends. In what ways have you experienced being a friend of the Lord?

How have you experienced being chosen by God?

READING

Acts 10:25–26, 34–35, 44–48

When Peter entered, Cornelius met him and, falling at his feet, paid him homage. Peter, however, raised him up, saying, "Get up. I myself am also a human being."

Then Peter proceeded to speak and said, "In truth, I see that God shows no partiality. Rather, in every nation whoever fears him and acts uprightly is acceptable to him."

While Peter was still speaking these things, the Holy Spirit fell upon all who were listening to the word. The circumcised believers who had accompanied Peter were astounded that the gift of the Holy Spirit should have been poured out on the Gentiles also, for they could hear them speaking in tongues and glorifying God. Then Peter responded, "Can anyone withhold the water for baptizing these people, who have received the Holy Spirit even as we have?" He ordered them to be baptized in the name of Jesus Christ.

REFLECTING

Who have been some of the Christians who opened your horizons? How have your experiences with them changed the way you think about what it means to be a Christian?

REMEMBERING

Up until that time, Peter never imagined that the message of Jesus would change the hearts of anyone but his fellow Israelites. It wasn't until he experienced the faith of a Gentile, Cornelius, that Peter's own horizons were opened.

PRAYING

Spend a few minutes in prayer, thanking God for those whose final farewells have given you hope, encouraged you, enlightened you. Thank God for those specific people whose words or actions have opened horizons for you. Ask God for the grace you need to be such a person for others.

The Ascension of the Lord

REMEMBERING

We begin by remembering. We remember events long ago and not so long ago. We remember how the story began and how it ended. It may have been a story we read, a story we heard, or a story we watched. It may have been a true story, a story of events that really happened, or a story of fiction that somehow communicated a truth that made the story worth remembering.

We remember stories we've told ourselves, as well as stories we've heard from others. Sometimes the words themselves are memorable. Sometimes the event that is described stays with us still. Sometimes it's what wasn't said or revealed that leaves us wondering, that triggers our imaginations, that makes us want to know what else happened.

READING

Year A
Matthew 28:16–20

The eleven disciples went to Galilee, to the mountain to which Jesus had ordered them. When they saw him, they worshiped, but they doubted. Then Jesus approached and said to them, "All power in heaven and on earth has been given to me. Go, therefore, and make disciples of all nations, baptizing them in the name of the Father, and of the Son, and of the Holy Spirit, teaching them to observe all that I have commanded you. And behold, I am with you always, until the end of the age."

Year B
Mark 16:15–20

Jesus said to his disciples: "Go into the whole world and proclaim the gospel to every creature. Whoever believes and is baptized will be saved; whoever does not believe will be condemned. These signs will accompany those who believe: in my name they will drive out demons, they will speak new languages. They will pick up serpents with their hands, and if they drink any deadly thing, it will not harm them. They will lay hands on the sick, and they will recover."

So then the Lord Jesus, after he spoke to them, was taken up into heaven and took his seat at the right hand of God. But they went forth and preached everywhere, while the Lord worked with them and confirmed the word through accompanying signs.

Year C
Luke 24:46–53

Jesus said to his disciples: "Thus it is written that the Christ would suffer and rise from the dead on the third day and that repentance, for the forgiveness of sins, would be preached in his name to all the nations, beginning from Jerusalem. You are witnesses of these things. And behold I am sending the promise of my Father upon you; but stay in the city until you are clothed with power from on high."

Then he led them out as far as Bethany, raised his hands, and blessed them. As he blessed them he parted from them and was taken up to heaven. They did him homage and then returned to Jerusalem with great joy, and they were continually in the temple praising God.

REMEMBERING

Today we hear the end of the story. The end of the Gospels—the final event in the life of Jesus among us—is proclaimed. His final instructions to his disciples are read.

They gathered with the Master, who had died and was risen. It was to be the last time Jesus appeared to them. His final words would be like a last will and testament—a final instruction on the meaning of discipleship. In each of the three Gospel accounts of the Ascension, Jesus sends his disciples to proclaim the good news, to tell the whole world the good news. The story ends with a command to remember the story and repeat it over and over again until everyone has heard it.

There is an old story about what happened in heaven immediately after the Ascension. Jesus is met by several angels as he returns to heaven. They ask him what will happen next. He tells them how the world will be transformed into the kingdom of God. One of the angels asks him how this will happen. He tells them about his followers and how they will spread the message and complete the mission he has begun. One of the angels then asks, "What's your Plan B?" The angel doesn't seem to believe that the followers of Jesus can or will continue the mission Jesus began.

St. Teresa of Ávila once had a vision of the Lord. In it Jesus stands before her, but he has no hands, and he says only this: I have no hands but yours now!

REFLECTING

Who are some of the people who have carried out the mission of Jesus in your life, who have been the hands of Christ in our world today?

What can you do to continue the mission of Jesus? How can you be the hands of Christ today, tomorrow, the rest of this week, and throughout your life?

READING

Acts of the Apostles 1:1–11

In the first book, Theophilus, I dealt with all that Jesus did and taught until the day he was taken up, after giving instructions through the Holy Spirit to the apostles whom he had chosen. He presented himself alive to them by many proofs after he had suffered, appearing to them during forty days and speaking about the kingdom of God. While meeting with them, he enjoined them not to depart from Jerusalem, but to wait for "the promise of the Father about which you have heard me speak; for John baptized with water, but in a few days you will be baptized with the Holy Spirit."

When they had gathered together they asked him, "Lord, are you at this time going to restore the kingdom to Israel?" He answered them, "It is not for you to know the times or seasons that the Father has established by his own authority. But you will receive power when the Holy Spirit comes upon you, and you will be my witnesses in Jerusalem, throughout Judea and Samaria, and to the ends of the earth." When he had said this, as they were looking on, he was lifted up, and a cloud took him from their sight. While they were looking intently at the sky as he was going, suddenly two men dressed in white garments stood beside them. They said, "Men of Galilee, why are you standing there looking at the sky? This Jesus who has been taken up from you into heaven will return in the same way as you have seen him going into heaven."

REMEMBERING

Remember what was said as you were confirmed, anointed with sacred chrism at the Easter Vigil. Just before the laying on of hands, you heard these words:

> The promised strength of the Holy Spirit, which you are to receive, will make you more like Christ and help you to be witnesses of his suffering, death, and resurrection. It will strengthen you to be active members of the Church and to build up the Body of Christ in faith and love.

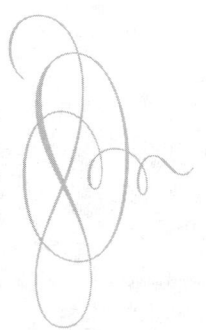

PRAYING

Give thanks to God for those who have continued the mission of Christ and helped you to know of your salvation. Then ask God for the grace you need to carry out that mission in your life, to be the hands of Christ in the world today, to be a witness of the suffering, death, and resurrection of Christ.

REFLECTING

The apostles' immediate response to Jesus' command was merely to stand there staring at the sky, when "suddenly two men dressed in white garments stood beside them." They admonished the apostles to stop standing there, doing nothing. "Get back to Jerusalem. You've got a job to do!" were their basic instructions.

Who have been some of those who have challenged you to stop staring at the sky and get on with the work of being "witnesses of his suffering, death, and resurrection"? How can you be such witnesses?

St. Francis of Assisi is said to have told his followers, "Preach always! If necessary use words!" There are many ways to be witnesses of the suffering, death, and resurrection of Christ. Not all of them require the use of words. How have you witnessed? How can you witness?
What will you do this week to witness to the suffering, death, and resurrection of Christ?

7th Sunday of Easter

REMEMBERING

We begin by remembering. We remember events long ago and not so long ago. We remember being prayed for. We might remember being prayed for as a child by a parent, grandparent, neighbor, or friend. We might remember someone saying that they would pray for us when we were facing a particularly challenging situation. We may remember being prayed for by one other person in a very private setting or being prayed for by a large group of people in a more public place.

We probably remember what it was like being prayed for at the Rite of Acceptance, the Rite of Election, the Scrutinies, and at the Easter Vigil. We may remember hearing prayers offered for the neophytes during the prayers of the faithful at Mass every Sunday since Easter.

How did it feel the first time you can remember someone offering to pray for you? How did it feel when you were prayed for by name in the midst of the parish gathered at Mass? What was it like to be prayed for by the bishop in a gathering with other catechumens from throughout the diocese?

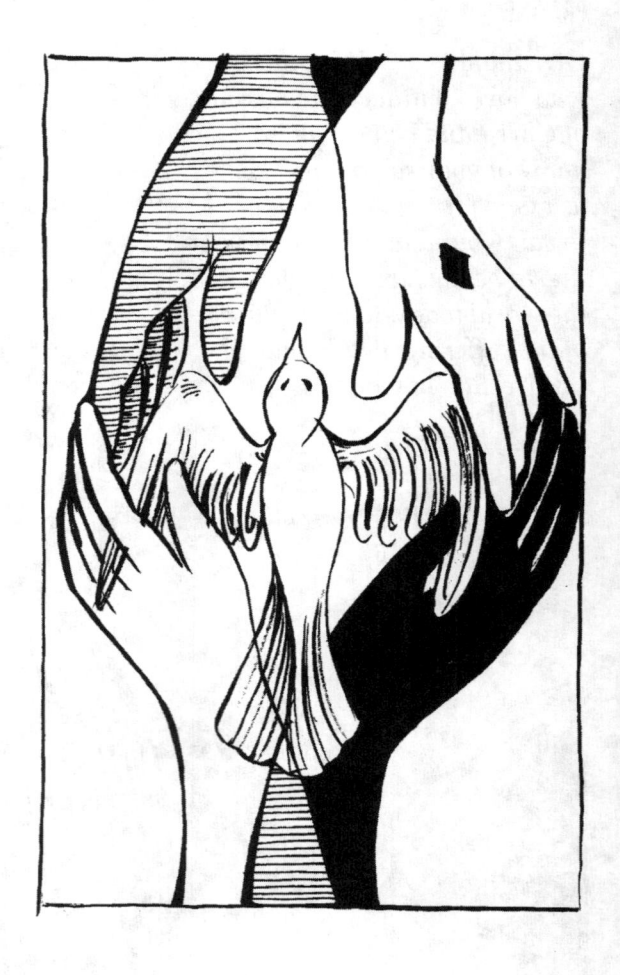

READING

Each year on this Sunday, we read only part of Jesus' prayer for the disciples and for those who will believe because of their preaching. It would be good for us to read the entire prayer at this time.

John 17:1–26

Jesus raised his eyes to heaven and said, "Father, the hour has come. Give glory to your son, so that your son may glorify you, just as you gave him authority over all people, so that your son may give eternal life to all you gave him. Now this is eternal life, that they should know you, the only true God, and the one whom you sent, Jesus Christ. I glorified you on earth by accomplishing the work that you gave me to do. Now glorify me, Father, with you, with the glory that I had with you before the world began.

"I revealed your name to those whom you gave me out of the world. They belonged to you, and you gave them to me, and they have kept your word. Now they know that everything you gave me is from you, because the words you gave to me I have given to them, and they accepted them and truly understood that I came from you, and they have believed that you sent me. I pray for them. I do not pray for the world but for the ones you have given me, because they are yours, and everything of mine is yours and everything of yours is mine, and I have been glorified in them. And now I will no longer be in the world, but they are in the world, while I am coming to you. Holy Father, keep them in your name that you have given me, so that they may be one just as we are one. When I was with them I protected them in your name that you gave me, and I guarded them, and none of them was lost except the son of destruction, in order that the Scripture might be fulfilled. But now I am coming to you. I speak this in the world so that they may share my joy completely. I gave them your word, and the world hated them, because they do not belong to the world any more than I belong to the world. I do not ask that you take them out of the world but that you keep them from the evil one. They do not belong to the world any more than I belong to the world. Consecrate them in the truth. Your word is truth. As you sent me into the world, so I sent them into the world. And I consecrate myself for them, so that they also may be consecrated in truth.

"Holy Father, I pray not only for them, but also for those who will believe in me through their word, so that they may all be one, as you, Father, are in me and I in you, that they also may be in us, that the world may believe that you sent me. And I have given them the glory you gave me, so that they may be one, as we are one, I in them and you in me, that they may be brought to perfection as one, that the world may know that you sent me, and that you loved them even as you loved me. Father, they are your gift to me. I wish that where I am they also may be with me, that they may see my glory that you gave me, because you loved me before the foundation of the world. Righteous Father, the world also does not know you, but I know you, and they know that you sent me. I made known to them your name and I will make it known, that the love with which you loved me may be in them and I in them."

REFLECTING

John's Gospel tells us that they gathered for a meal, just before Passover. Jesus washed their feet, instructed them to do as he had done, warned them of betrayals and denials that were about to come, and gave them a new commandment to love one another. He told them that he would be leaving soon and that where he was going they could not come. He promised to send the Advocate, the Holy Spirit, and he gave them the gift of peace. He told them that they were as close as a vine and its branches, that they were no longer slaves but friends, and that he would lay down his life for them. He also spoke of the Father, and then he spoke to the Father.

Imagine for a moment what it must have been like. Imagine their very mixed feelings of astonishment, bewilderment, confusion, denial, and exaltation. One moment they seemed delighted; the next they were close to despair. And then he prayed for them. He placed them in the hands of his heavenly Father.

This was not just a prayer for those in the room. It was a prayer for all his disciples, for those in the room then and for those who would come after them. It was—it is—a prayer for us, too. Jesus is praying for us, both personally and collectively.

Imagine that you are in that room and that Jesus is praying for you. Read the prayer again. Listen to it as Jesus prays for you.

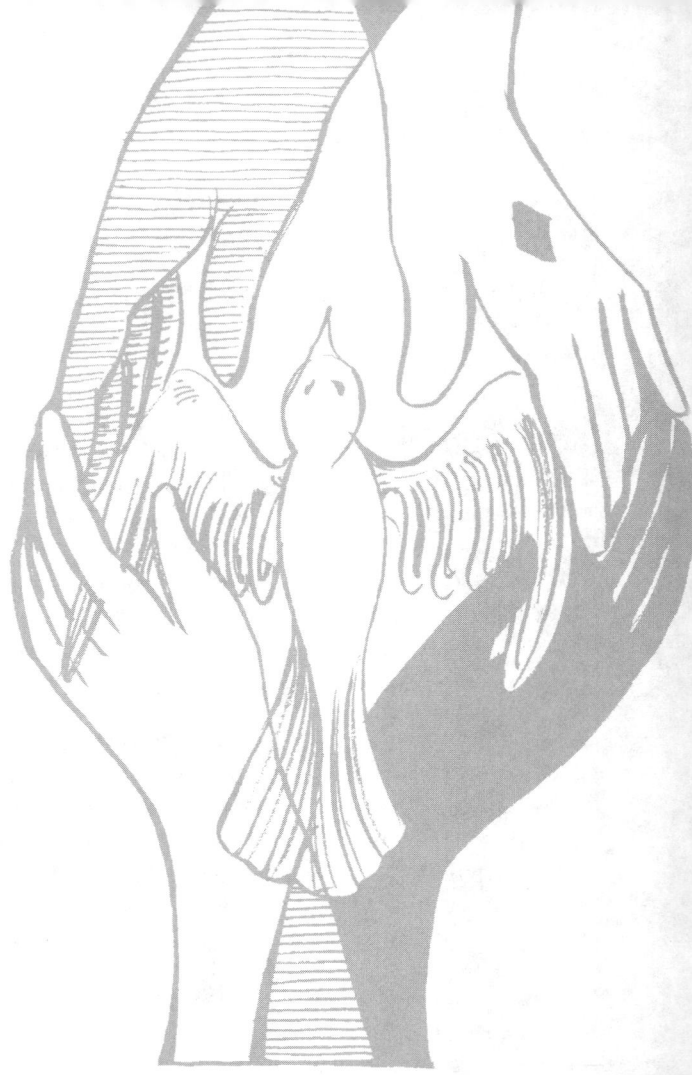

PRAYING

Thank Jesus for his prayer. Ask God for the graces you need for Christ's prayer to be fulfilled in you and in the world today.

Pentecost

The chrism used at the Easter Vigil might be present, as well as the Easter candle or the neophytes' baptismal candles.

REMEMBERING

We begin by remembering. We remember events long ago and not so long ago. We remember surprises and events long anticipated. We may remember waiting for the last day of school, a vacation trip, a visit from a friend or family member we had not seen for a long time. We remember long-awaited celebrations. We remember the anticipation. We remember the excitement building as the event or occasion drew near.

We might also remember how the actual event was experienced. Sometimes it was a little less exciting than we had anticipated. We experienced disappointment. Other times it was even more than we had hoped for or imagined.

Those gathered in the upper room had heard the promises—had believed the promises—made by Jesus when he was among them.

READING

John 14:15–16, 23b–26; 15:26–27; 16:12–15

Jesus said to his disciples: "If you love me, you will keep my commandments. And I will ask the Father, and he will give you another Advocate to be with you always.

"Whoever loves me will keep my word, and my Father will love him, and we will come to him and make our dwelling with him. Those who do not love me do not keep my words; yet the word you hear is not mine but that of the Father who sent me.

"I have told you this while I am with you. The Advocate, the Holy Spirit that the Father will send in my name, will teach you everything and remind you of all that I told you.

"When the Advocate comes whom I will send you from the Father, the Spirit of truth that proceeds from the Father, he will testify to me. And you also testify, because you have been with me from the beginning.

"I have much more to tell you, but you cannot bear it now. But when he comes, the Spirit of truth, he will guide you to all truth. He will not speak on his own, but he will speak what he hears, and will declare to you the things that are coming. He will glorify me, because he will take from what is mine and declare it to you. Everything that the Father has is mine; for this reason I told you that he will take from what is mine and declare it to you."

These were Jesus' promises, promises fulfilled more spectacularly than they had imagined.

Acts of the Apostles 2:1–4

When the time for Pentecost was fulfilled, they were all in one place together. And suddenly there came from the sky a noise like a strong driving wind, and it filled the entire house in which they were. Then there appeared to them tongues as of fire, which parted and came to rest on each one of them. And they were all filled with the Holy Spirit and began to speak in different tongues, as the Spirit enabled them to proclaim.

REFLECTING

Imagine what it must have been like. They had been waiting for some time. For forty days Jesus had been appearing to them from time to time. Then he was gone. For the next ten days they waited—first staring at the sky on the hilltop, then gathering together in Jerusalem. So often waiting is the worst part of any experience. It is the

REMEMBERING

How did you feel? You had waited quite some time. You had heard promises, maybe even some descriptions of what it would be like. Then it happened. The flame of faith was lit and divided. The water was poured, the oil rubbed onto your head. You were sealed with the gift of the Holy Spirit. You received the flame of faith.

Looking back over the past fifty days of joy, what do you remember about that wonderful night when you, like the disciples, waited for the Spirit's arrival? What do you remember about the experience of receiving the Spirit's gifts?

not knowing when or what exactly to expect that can be unnerving.

Were they gathered together peacefully in prayer as so many of the artistic renderings of the event seem to indicate? Or were they still arguing about who was the most important, what he meant when he said . . . . How long they should wait? Were they patient or impatient as they waited? Did some of them come and go, as they had done just after the Crucifixion, when Thomas left for a while only to return to discover that the Lord had appeared to the others while he was away?

And then suddenly it happened. The wind blew. The house shook. Tongues as of fire appeared and parted and came to rest on each of them. Were they excited, shocked, astonished, speechless, or shouting out in amazement and joy?

We will never know exactly what happened that day, but we can imagine. How would you have felt?

REMEMBERING

Once the gift of the Spirit was received, the disciples reacted.

READING

Acts of the Apostles 2:5–11

Now there were devout Jews from every nation under heaven staying in Jerusalem. At this sound, they gathered in a large crowd, but they were confused because each one heard them speaking in his own language. They were astounded, and in amazement they asked, "Are not all these people who are speaking Galileans? Then how does each of us hear them in his native language? We are Parthians, Medes, and Elamites, inhabitants of Mesopotamia, Judea and Cappadocia, Pontus and Asia, Phrygia and Pamphylia, Egypt and the districts of Libya near Cyrene, as well as travelers from Rome, both Jews and converts to Judaism, Cretans and Arabs, yet we hear them speaking in our own tongues of the mighty acts of God."

PRAYING

Give thanks to God for all that has happened over the past fifty days, all that has happened that led up to those days. Ask God for the grace you need to go forth as an apostle—as one sent by God to be a witness to the Resurrection.

REFLECTING

While you may not have spoken in such a way that all who heard you understood, has anything astonishing or amazing happened in your life since you received that Holy Spirit?